The Sales Parables

Timeless Tales for Modern Sales

Mike Martin

Mike Martin

Book Cover by Georgia Boon

First edition 2024

Contents

Chapter One

Where It All Began

Where It All Began

In the early days of mankind, when the world was still wild and untamed, survival was a daily struggle. The earth was vast, divided by mountains, rivers, and endless forests, each region holding its own secrets and dangers. In this harsh landscape, two tribes lived in wary proximity, separated by a turbulent river that cut through a valley rich with game and resources.

To the east, the Hawk Clan sharpened their flint-tipped spears, preparing for another hunt. They were a people of strength and precision, skilled in the art of the chase. Their warriors were formidable, their muscles hardened from years of stalking prey across open fields and dense forests. But despite their prowess, the Hawk Clan faced a problem they could not solve with spears alone. The herds they relied on for food were becoming scarce, the prey more elusive. Even their sharp eyes and quick feet could not guarantee a successful hunt. As the days passed, their stores of meat dwindled, and hunger gnawed at their bellies.

Across the river, the Wolf Tribe faced a different challenge. They were a clever, resourceful people, renowned for their skills in crafting traps and tools. They could snare rabbits and birds with ease, weaving nets and setting snares with a dexterity that rivaled the weaving of their baskets. Yet, for all their ingenuity, they were not warriors. Their flimsy weapons offered little protection against the predators that stalked the night, or against the stronger, fiercer tribes that roamed the land. Fear was their constant companion, and they longed for the strength to defend what they had built.

For many moons, the two tribes watched each other with suspicion. Each possessed something the other needed. The Hawks had strength, but lacked the skill to catch smaller, elusive game. The Wolves had cunning and tools, but lacked the means to protect themselves. The river, which could have been a bridge between them, had become a barrier of distrust. Both tribes considered crossing it, not to trade, but to take by force what they needed. War seemed inevitable, a conflict that would drain both tribes of what little they had left.

It was on the brink of this potential bloodshed that a stranger arrived in the valley. No one knew where he came from or how he had found his way to this remote place. He was a man of unassuming appearance, dressed in simple robes patched with different furs and fabrics, his face partly hidden by a tangle of beard. He carried with him a modest pack, filled not with weapons, but with curious objects—trinkets, tools, and small pieces of flint and metal.

He approached the riverbank with a calm, confident stride, his eyes taking in the two tribes gathered on either side. As he reached the edge of the water, he raised his hands in a gesture of peace and called out in a voice that carried across the rushing current. "People of the Hawk! People of the Wolf! I bring you a message—one of hope and opportunity!"

The tribesmen, startled by this intrusion, gathered at the water's edge. Chief Talon of the Hawk Clan, a broad-shouldered man with a fierce gaze, stepped forward. "Who are you, stranger, to speak of hope in a time of need?" he demanded. "We do not know you. Speak quickly, or leave."

The stranger inclined his head respectfully. "I am a traveler," he said. "I have journeyed far and seen many lands. I know the ways of men and the ways of the wild. I see your strength, Hawk Clan, and I see your wisdom, Wolf Tribe. But I also see your need. You both have something the other lacks. Why not exchange what you have, rather than fight for what you want?"

Elder Fang of the Wolf Tribe, a lean man with a sharp mind and a sharper tongue, frowned. "And what would we gain from this exchange? The Hawks are strong, yes, but they are no craftsmen. What could they possibly offer us that we cannot make ourselves?"

The stranger smiled, his eyes twinkling with a light that spoke of understanding and perhaps something more. "Strength, Elder Fang. Protection. The Hawk Clan can guard your camps, defend your people from the dangers that lurk in the dark. In return, you can teach them the art of crafting traps, the skill of catching what eludes their spears. Together, you can be stronger than you are apart."

The tribes murmured amongst themselves, the idea strange and unfamiliar, yet intriguing. Chief Talon glanced at his warriors, their faces lined with the strain of hunger. "And why should we trust them, traveler?" he asked. "We have fought before. We have bled and lost. Why should we believe that this time will be different?"

"Because this time," the stranger replied, "you have me. I will stand as the bridge between you, a neutral voice, a guarantor of fairness. I will oversee the exchange, ensure that each side keeps its word. I ask for nothing more than a fair portion of what you gain—a small share to sustain my travels."

Elder Fang's eyes narrowed. "And if you deceive us? What then?"

The stranger's expression remained calm, his voice steady. "If I deceive you, you may cast me out, or worse. But I have no desire to deceive. I seek only to bring balance where there is discord, to build where others would destroy."

A heavy silence settled over the valley as the tribes considered his words. Finally, Chief Talon spoke, his voice grudging but respectful. "We will listen, traveler. Meet us at the old oak at sunset. We will hear more of your plan."

Elder Fang nodded in agreement. "Agreed. But know this—we come with open hands, but we will not be fools."

And so, under the great branches of the old oak that stood alone near the river's bend, the first negotiation took place. The stranger guided the tribes through their initial exchange. The Hawks, now equipped with traps, quickly learned to catch the smaller game that had eluded them. The Wolves, under the Hawks' watchful guard, slept easier, their fears of nightly predators and rival raiders easing. For the first time in many moons, both tribes found themselves not at odds, but in cooperation. They began to see each other not as rivals, but as partners.

Weeks passed, and the results were undeniable. The Hawks grew stronger and more skilled, their children no longer crying from hunger. The Wolves, feeling secure, turned their creative minds to other tasks, building better tools and even improving the Hawks' weapons. Prosperity began to bloom where only conflict had been.

The stranger continued his work, moving between the two camps, always with a smile, always with a keen eye for opportunity. He suggested new ideas, new ways to work together, always seeking a balance that would benefit both sides. His presence became a welcome one, his words a source of guidance and wisdom.

And as the tribes prospered, word of their success spread beyond the valley. Other tribes, hearing of this new way of living, came to see for themselves. They, too, sought the stranger's help, eager to exchange what they had for what they needed. The stranger, ever adaptable, guided them, brokered deals, and established agreements that brought peace where there had been conflict.

In time, his influence grew, reaching far beyond the valley. He became a legend, a figure known not for his strength or his skill with a weapon, but for his ability to see what others could not—the potential for cooperation, the power of exchange. He had brought something new to the world, something that transcended the old ways of war and conquest.

And thus, it was said that this man, this traveler who walked between tribes and brought them together, possessed the most valuable skill of all. For he did not hunt, nor did he fight. He did not craft weapons or traps, nor did he build huts or boats. What he offered was a vision, a way forward that could transform enemies into allies, scarcity into abundance, conflict into progress.

He was not merely a man of words, but a man of action—a man who understood that the greatest power lay not in taking, but in giving, not in war, but in negotiation, not in isolation, but in connection.

And so, with every deal he made, every agreement he brokered, he shaped the future of mankind, pushing them from their primitive shelters toward the dawn of civilisation. For he knew that without this skill, there could be no advancement, no peace, no prosperity.

He was, in essence, the first of his kind. A true innovator. A master of his craft. The one who brought about the first exchange, who understood the value of every word and every gesture.

And only in the end, as he walked away from the valley that now thrived because of his influence, did they realise what he truly was: a salesman.

Lesson: "See beyond the immediate need; find the win-win opportunity."

Chapter Two

The Power of Giving

The Power of Giving

Gregory McDonald, known to his mates as Mac, had been pounding the pavement for years. His trade was selling coffee machines to offices across London. But as Mac knew all too well, the real money wasn't in the machines themselves—it was in getting customers to sign up for monthly coffee subscriptions. The machines were a one-off sale; the coffee kept the cash flowing.

Mac had a simple enough pitch: "Buy our machines, and you'll never have to worry about coffee again." He would spend his days darting from one office to another, lugging his trusty demonstration model behind him, and delivering the same spiel. But no matter how many appointments he booked, he was failing to close the deals.

"I just don't get it," he muttered to himself one evening, slumping into his chair at the kitchen table. The dining room light flickered slightly, casting shadows over his furrowed brow. Isabel, his wife, looked up from the dishes she was drying and noticed the frustration etched across his face.

"Rough day?" she asked softly, setting down the dish towel.

"Rough month," Mac replied with a sigh. "I've been getting loads of appointments, but every time I walk out, I'm empty-handed. The machines are top quality, but people just aren't buying them. And even if they do, they never go for the coffee subscription. It's like I'm speaking to a brick wall."

Isabel thought for a moment. "Well, if I were in their shoes, I wouldn't buy a machine without knowing what kind of coffee it makes. And if you were coming to sell me the machine, I'd want to try the coffee first."

Mac's eyes lit up. "You'd want to try the coffee first?"

"Of course," Isabel said, smiling. "You're selling the experience, Mac, not just a machine. People want to know what they're getting. And besides, nobody buys what they don't taste and love first."

That night, Mac couldn't sleep. Isabel's words kept ringing in his ears. "People want to know what they're getting." He stared at the ceiling, the solution slowly forming in his mind. He needed a different approach. Something that would make these office managers feel invested in the coffee before he even stepped through the door.

The next morning, Mac sprang out of bed with a newfound energy. He grabbed a notepad and started scribbling down his plan. As soon as he booked an appointment, he'd send a letter to the prospective client—a small gesture of goodwill. But that wasn't all. For five days before the meeting, he'd send ten cups of coffee to the office. One for the client and nine for their team. Each day, a different blend. The goal? To get them hooked on the coffee even before he tried to sell the machine.

When Isabel came downstairs, Mac had already made breakfast and was grinning from ear to ear. "I've got it," he said, sliding a cup of freshly brewed coffee towards her.

"Got what?" Isabel asked, amused by his sudden burst of enthusiasm.

"Reciprocity," he replied. "I'm going to give them something first—a taste of what they're missing. It's like you said, love. They need to try it before they buy it."

Over the next few weeks, Mac put his plan into action. As soon as an appointment was confirmed, he sent out a friendly letter, thanking the office manager for their time and promising to make their next coffee break special. Then, he arranged for ten cups of coffee to be delivered every day for five days leading up to the meeting—each day a different flavour. By the time Mac walked into those offices, the smell of fresh coffee had already made a name for itself.

When the day of his first appointment under the new plan arrived, Mac was nervous but determined. He walked into the office with his head held high and his demo machine ready, but he wasn't planning on using it—not right away, at least.

The office manager, Sarah, greeted him with a warm smile. "Gregory! Or should I call you Mac? Thanks for the coffee this week; it's been the talk of the office!" she exclaimed.

Mac chuckled, relieved to see the plan was working. "Call me Mac, please. And I'm glad to hear it! So, tell me, Sarah, which was your favourite?"

She thought for a moment. "I think I liked the Colombian blend the best. And the team's been raving about the Ethiopian dark roast."

Mac nodded. "Excellent choices. Both of those blends are perfect matches for our deluxe machine, the Model X5. It's designed to bring out the unique flavours of those beans."

Sarah looked intrigued. "Really? I've got to say, the coffee's been fantastic. But what about the machine?"

"Well, I could go on about the features and benefits," Mac said, leaning in slightly, "but you've already tasted the results. The Model X5 is the secret behind that rich, smooth Colombian blend you loved. And it's built to keep delivering that quality cup after cup."

By the end of the meeting, Mac wasn't just selling a machine; he was selling an experience, and Sarah was eager to buy in. But he wasn't done yet. "And the best part?" he added, "We can arrange for a monthly delivery of those exact blends. You won't have to lift a finger."

Sarah nodded, excitement in her eyes. "Let's do it. Let's get the machine and the coffee. Our team deserves it."

Mac walked out of that office with his first full sale in weeks—a machine and a coffee subscription. As he closed the door behind him, he couldn't help but smile. Isabel was right. It wasn't just about the product; it was about creating a sense of value, of giving before asking.

The orders started rolling in, and with each one, Mac's confidence grew. He realised the true power of reciprocity. By giving first, he created a sense of obligation—a subtle but powerful push in the right direction. And as a result, his sales soared.

That evening, as he sat down to dinner with Isabel and their daughters, Mac felt a sense of accomplishment he hadn't felt in months. He raised his glass of water. "To reciprocity," he toasted. "And to always giving before asking."

Isabel laughed and raised her own glass. "And to coffee," she added with a wink.

They all laughed, clinking their glasses together. Mac realised he wasn't just selling machines or coffee; he was building relationships, one cup at a time. And that made all the difference.

Lessons:

Give Before You Ask: Providing value upfront creates a sense of obligation and goodwill, making prospects more receptive to your offer.

Sell the Experience, Not Just the Product: Demonstrating the benefits of your product through real experiences helps customers see its value more clearly.

Create a Sense of Value: Show potential customers what they stand to gain, not just what you want to sell them.

Build Relationships: Focus on building trust and relationships, which often leads to better sales outcomes than a hard sell approach.

Chapter Three

It Must Be Mine

It Must Be Mine

Winston Bredbury stood behind the polished oak counter of his small London boutique, lost in thought. The scent of fine leather and expensive cologne filled the air, mingling with the soft notes of jazz playing from hidden speakers. His shop was filled with meticulously crafted Italian suits, each one a masterpiece of tailoring. Yet, for all their quality, they weren't selling for as much as he'd hoped. Winston wanted more than just to sell suits; he wanted to sell luxury. He dreamed of clients paying tens of thousands, not just a few thousand.

He glanced at the invoice in his hand—a custom suit sold to a wealthy entrepreneur for £4,000. "Four grand," he muttered, shaking his head. It was good money, sure, but not the kind of money that would set his boutique apart. He knew his suits were worth more—they were made from the finest materials, tailored to perfection. But his clients, despite their wealth, saw them as just another suit.

"What am I missing?" Winston mumbled to himself. He was sure there was a way to elevate his offerings, to make his suits not just garments, but statements. But how? He needed a spark, an idea that would transform the way his clients perceived his products.

That evening, Winston sat in his kitchen, watching his wife Pam prepare dinner. The sound of their two sons playing football in the garden drifted in through the open window. Pam, a social psychologist, had a knack for understanding people, and Winston hoped she could help him understand his clients a bit better tonight.

"Pam," he began, breaking the silence. "I need your help with something. It's about my suits."

Pam turned from the stove, her eyes curious. "Go on, I'm listening."

"I want to sell my suits for more—much more. I'm talking tens of thousands. But I don't know how to make that leap. How do you make something so valuable that people will pay a premium for it?"

Pam smiled, a knowing look on her face. "Funny you should ask. I just spent £1,000 on a football shirt for our son."

Winston's eyes widened. "A thousand pounds? On a football shirt?"

Pam laughed. "Yes, but it's not just any football shirt. It's signed by David Beckham. There's only one like it."

Winston blinked, surprised. "You spent a grand because it's signed by Beckham?"

Pam nodded. "Exactly. It's unique, Winston. It's one-of-a-kind. That's what makes it valuable."

Winston sat back, a smile slowly forming on his lips. "Unique...scarcity... That's it!" he exclaimed, his eyes lighting up with excitement. "That's what I need to do with my suits! I need to make them unique. I need to create scarcity."

Pam grinned. "Now you're on to something. It's all about perception. People are willing to pay a lot more for something if they believe it's rare, special—one-of-a-kind."

Winston nodded, his mind now racing with possibilities. "But how do I make my suits truly unique? They're already custom-made."

"Think beyond just the fabric and the fit," Pam suggested. "Think about what you can add to make each suit a unique experience, a story. Something that makes it more than just a piece of clothing."

That night, Winston stayed up late, scribbling down ideas. The next morning, he called his supplier in Italy to inquire about the rarest, most exotic fabrics they could source. He spoke to a renowned London jeweller about incorporating precious stones into bespoke buttons and cufflinks. He even reached out to an artist who specialised in custom embroidery for the linings, offering personalised messages or initials in delicate, hand-stitched patterns. He was determined to make each suit as unique and desirable as Beckham's signed football shirt.

Within a week, Winston had created his first "Signature Collection" suit. It was made from rare cashmere sourced from the Himalayas, with mother-of-pearl buttons and a silk lining hand-embroidered with a personal message in gold thread. It wasn't just a suit—it was a masterpiece.

He decided to showcase this new creation to his wealthiest client, Mr. Harrison, a tech mogul known for his love of exclusivity. Winston invited him to a private viewing at the boutique. As Harrison entered, Winston led him to a secluded fitting room where the suit was displayed under soft, ambient lighting.

"What do you think, Mr. Harrison?" Winston asked, his voice calm, though his heart was pounding with anticipation.

Harrison's eyes widened as he examined the suit. "This...this is extraordinary," he murmured, running his fingers over the fabric. "I've never seen anything like it."

Winston smiled. "That's because there isn't anything like it, Mr. Harrison. This suit is made from the rarest materials, with bespoke details like these mother-of-pearl buttons and a hand-embroidered lining that can bear any message or initials of your choosing. It's not just a suit—it's a statement, an experience that's unique to you."

Harrison nodded slowly, clearly impressed. "And how much does this unique experience cost?"

Winston took a deep breath. "This one-of-a-kind piece is priced at £30,000."

To his surprise and delight, Harrison didn't hesitate. "I'll take it," he said with a grin. "And I think I'll order another one for my son's graduation. Something that's uniquely his."

Winston felt a surge of triumph. He had done it. He had turned something ordinary into something extraordinary by creating scarcity and uniqueness. His suits were no longer just clothing; they were symbols of exclusivity and prestige.

Over the following months, word spread about Winston's boutique. Clients began to see his suits not just as attire, but as personal investments—unique pieces that reflected their own tastes and status. Sales skyrocketed, and Winston finally felt like he had unlocked a secret he had been searching for all along.

As he closed the shop one evening, he reflected on the lesson he had learned. It wasn't enough to sell something of high quality. To command a higher price, it had to be more than just good—it had to be rare, special, and truly one-of-a-kind. Scarcity wasn't just a sales tactic; it was a powerful tool in the art of selling.

And all it took was a signed football shirt to make him see it.

Winston realised that creating scarcity and uniqueness was not just about raising prices, but about transforming the way clients perceived value. It wasn't about the suits themselves; it was about making every customer feel like they were getting something truly special—something no one else could have. And that made all the difference.

Lesson: To command a higher price, it's not enough to offer a high-quality product; it must be perceived as rare and unique. When people believe they're getting something exclusive, they're willing to pay more. Transform your product into a one-of-a-kind experience, and watch its value soar.

Chapter Four

The Cool Kids Strategy

The Cool Kids Strategy

D aniel Bolder, known as Dan to his friends, was pacing back and forth in his small shop in Manchester, frustration etched across his face. The shelves were neatly lined with his own trainer brand, Spinoff—sports trainers designed specifically for athletes. They were sleek, stylish, and made from the finest materials. But none of that seemed to matter. Sales were dismal.

"Why isn't anyone buying these?" Dan muttered to himself, looking around at the empty store. He had tried everything he could think of. He'd sold them at local markets, set up an online store, even placed them in a few local shops. Yet, no matter what he did, it felt like he was shouting into the void. The trainers were expensive, yes, but they were worth every penny. So why couldn't he convince anyone else of that?

The bills were piling up, and Dan's small warehouse at the back of his shop was still filled with boxes of unsold trainers. Every day, he felt the pressure mounting, like a noose tightening around his neck. He had poured his heart and soul into Spinoff, and now it seemed like it was all for nothing. He could feel his dream slipping away, piece by piece.

One evening, after yet another fruitless day, Dan found himself at the local bar, drowning his sorrows in a pint. He was joined by his friend Simon and Simon's teenage son, Mark. Dan sighed heavily, recounting his woes.

"I've tried everything, mate," Dan said, shaking his head. "Online, offline, in shops, in markets—nothing works. No one's buying my trainers."

Simon listened sympathetically, but it was Mark who piped up with an unexpected insight. "You know why no one's buying them?" he asked. Dan looked at him, a bit startled. "Because no one gives a shit about your trainers, mate."

Dan's eyes widened, feeling a sting. "Cheers for that, lad," he muttered, feeling even worse.

"No, seriously," Mark continued. "It's not about the trainers themselves. It's about who's wearing them. If none of the cool kids are wearing them, no one's going to want them. You get the cool kids, you get everyone. That's how it works."

Dan stopped and thought about it. Mark was right. Kids followed trends, and trends were set by those deemed the 'cool kids'. If he could get them to wear his trainers, the rest would follow.

That night, Dan lay awake, thinking about Mark's words. By morning, he had a plan. It was bold, maybe even a little crazy, but he had nothing to lose.

Dan hired a few young people to stand outside every school within a five-mile radius of his shop, asking the same questions to every child who left the school gates: "Who is the coolest kid in this school? Who is the coolest girl? Who is the coolest boy?" They were simple questions, but they were the key to everything.

For a week, the answers poured in. Every day, Dan reviewed the data, carefully compiling a list of names. By the end of the week, he had a solid list of the fifteen coolest kids in the area. These were the kids who could make or break a trend with just a nod of approval.

Dan reached out to these kids through their schools. He made them a proposition they couldn't refuse. "How would you like to make £200 a week for a month and get a pair of Spinoff trainers in every colour?" he asked them. There was just one rule: they couldn't tell anyone about the arrangement, and they had to wear the trainers all the time.

Ten kids took him up on the offer. Ten of the coolest kids in the area, each of them now sporting a different pair of Spinoffs every day. And then, something amazing happened.

Within days, Dan noticed a change. Kids were coming into his shop, asking for the trainers they'd seen their mates wearing. "Do you have the ones like Jake's?" "Can I get the pink ones like Emma's?" Word spread like wildfire. The cool kids were wearing Spin-offs, and suddenly, everyone wanted a pair.

Sales exploded. Dan's small shop was buzzing with activity. The warehouse that had once been a symbol of his failure was now a hive of activity, with boxes coming in and out at a breakneck pace. Orders were pouring in, not just locally but from all over the UK. Online sales skyrocketed. Dan could barely keep up with demand.

Within a few months, Dan had sold thousands of pairs of trainers. His brand, which had been on the brink of collapse, was now one of the hottest names in athletic footwear. He had cracked the code. The secret wasn't just in having a good product; it was about social proof. It was about getting the right people to wear your product and letting the rest of the market follow.

As Dan stood in his shop, watching customers stream in, he thought back to that night in the bar and Mark's words. The kid had been right all along. You get the cool kids, you get everyone.

And with a smile, Dan realised he had turned his little brand into something much bigger. He had created a movement, all by understanding the power of social proof. And now, there was no stopping him.

The lesson was clear: sometimes, it's not about what you're selling but who's buying.

Lesson: Don't just focus on the features of your product; focus on its visibility. Identify the trendsetters in your market and get them on your side. When the right people are seen using your product, others will naturally follow. Remember, it's not always about what you're selling; it's about who's buying.

Chapter Five

Why Should Anyone Listen To You?

Why Should Anyone Listen To You?

B rian Thompson was on top of the world—or so he thought. With a name that resonated in online business circles, he had built and sold three seven-figure companies in just five years, topping it all off with an $8 million sale. People who knew Brian were in awe of his achievements. They hung onto his every word, taking notes and nodding along as if he were the modern-day prophet of digital entrepreneurship.

Brian's transition from business builder to speaker seemed like a natural next step. He had mastered the art of making money online and figured it was time to teach others how to do the same. His pitch was simple: learn how to grow your online business to seven figures, sell it, pocket the money, and walk away. Or, if you fancied a longer game, scale it up to eight figures over a few years. It was an enticing proposition, and Brian knew it.

For months, he toiled over his stage presentation. He packed it with every tip, trick, and strategy he'd ever used. He crafted clever leading questions designed to have the audience nodding along, agreeing with him every step of the way. His one-hour speech was honed to perfection, tested across multiple stages worldwide.

But now, he found himself in a dimly lit back room at yet another event, staring at his dismal sales numbers. He had given the presentation his all, yet again. And yet again, he was outsold by the other speakers—people with far less experience, less impressive backgrounds, and, in his mind, far less to offer.

Sitting beside him, Keith, an older man with silver hair and a weathered face, had been observing Brian closely. Keith was a veteran of the stage, with over 25 years of experience selling from the podium. He had seen it all—the good, the bad, and the downright awful. Keith had seen Brian speak before, and he knew exactly what was wrong.

Keith leaned forward and asked a simple question, his voice soft yet firm. "Brian, are you struggling to sell from the stage?"

Brian, slouched in his chair and gazing at the ground, nodded. "Yeah, I am. I don't get it. I've done everything right. Why aren't people buying?"

Keith looked at him for a moment, then asked, "Why should anybody listen to you?"

Brian's head snapped up. "Do you not know who I am?"

Keith shook his head. "No, never heard of you before. And why would anyone in the audience care or even listen to you?"

Brian felt a flash of anger. How could this man not know who he was? He launched into a rant. "I built my first business at 18. Sold it two years later for $300,000. In the last five years, I've built three seven-figure companies, sold them all for seven figures, and one for $8.3 million. I've got a master's degree in business, a PhD, and I'm the most qualified person on stage. I've had more success than all the other speakers combined! I'm the richest person at this event by a mile. People should want to listen to me!"

Keith smiled gently. "And you say all that at the beginning of your presentation?"

Brian blinked. "What?"

Keith leaned back in his chair, folding his arms. "When people see your presentation, they like it. They think you're clever, and you're good at what you do. But here's the thing: they don't know who you are, and more importantly, they don't know why they should care. You have no authority, Brian. There's no reason for them to believe a single word you're saying. They don't trust you. And that's why they don't buy."

Brian stared at him, his mind racing. He had thought his reputation preceded him, that his presence on stage was enough. But now, it dawned on him that Keith was right. Most of the people in the audience had never heard of him before they sat down. Why should they trust him over the next person?

Keith continued, "Start your presentation by establishing your authority. Explain to the people in the audience exactly why they should listen to you. Tell them about your achievements, your experience, your qualifications. Build that trust right from the start. Without authority, you're just another guy with a nice PowerPoint."

It was as if a light bulb had gone off in Brian's head. He had been so focused on the content, on delivering value, that he had forgotten one crucial element: authority. He realised he needed to start every presentation by giving people a reason to believe in him.

That night, Brian rewrote the opening of his speech. He didn't change a word of the content; he knew it was strong. But he began with a few minutes about his journey—his successes, his struggles, his qualifications. He made sure the audience knew exactly who he was and why he was worth listening to.

The next day, he took the stage with renewed confidence. He opened with his new introduction, laying out his credentials and sharing his story. He saw heads nodding, not just in agreement but in recognition. People leaned forward in their seats, intrigued and eager to hear more. By the end of the presentation, when it was time for the pitch, he could feel the room was with him. When the sales numbers came in, he had outsold every other speaker by a wide margin.

As he stepped off the stage, Keith was waiting for him, a knowing smile on his face. "Better?" he asked.

Brian grinned. "Much better. You were right. Authority changes everything."

Keith chuckled. "Welcome to the world of sales, Brian. It's not just what you say, it's who you are when you say it."

And with that, Brian learned one of the most important lessons in sales: Authority is not given. It's earned, built, and used to create trust. And without trust, there is no sale.

Lesson: Always begin by establishing your authority. Share your journey, your achievements, and your credentials upfront. Make sure your audience knows why they should listen to you and why you're the expert they need. Without authority, even the best sales pitch can fall flat. Build trust first, and the sales will follow.

"In sales, it's not just about what you say; it's about who you are when you say it." **Mike Martin**

Chapter Six

I Do What I Say I Will

I Do What I Say I Will

Mike Weinberg was a seasoned government sales representative. He'd seen it all, from pushing energy-efficient refrigerators to convincing city councils to embrace solar panels. But this new task was proving to be his most challenging yet. The council had tasked him with converting all the industrial estates in Greater Manchester to greener lighting solutions. The mission was simple: replace the high-energy-consuming lights with more sustainable options. But simple didn't mean easy.

Mike's job was to travel across the Northwest, speaking at packed events filled with business owners who were either tenants or landlords of commercial properties on these estates. The current lighting systems were not only outdated but were also significant contributors to global warming. They guzzled energy and cost a fortune to maintain. Mike had to make these business owners see the light—literally.

He put together what he thought was a compelling talk. He laid out the numbers, detailing how much these high-energy lights were costing them each year. He showed them the math: switch to greener lighting, spend a few thousand upfront, and in five to ten years, they'd be saving significant money. He even made a passionate appeal to their sense of right and wrong, stressing the importance of making a choice that was good for the planet.

But meeting after meeting, his efforts fell flat. Hundreds of tenants and commercial property owners, from all over Greater Manchester, listened politely, sipped their free coffee, and nibbled on biscuits. And yet, not a single one converted. It was as if they were all politely ignoring the elephant in the room.

After several weeks of this, Mike was exhausted and frustrated. He trudged back to the council office, ready to admit defeat. "Look, David," he said to one of the council leaders, "I've done everything I can. Nobody's interested. They don't care about the cost savings, and they definitely don't care about the environment. They're not going to switch to greener lighting. I think we need to scrap the idea and focus on something else. I'm tired of going from place to place, trying to sell this when nobody's buying."

David listened quietly, then raised a hand to stop him. "Mike, I hear you, but I'm not sure we've thought this through entirely. Let's get some fresh perspective. Sandra, could you come in here for a minute?"

Sandra, David's PA, entered the room. She was a petite woman in her early fifties, with a calm demeanour and sharp eyes that missed nothing. David introduced her and added, "Sandra has a degree in social psychology. She once told me about the principle of consistency, a psychological tactic great for getting people on board and changing their minds. It's worked for me in council speeches. Let's see if it can help here."

David explained the problem to Sandra, while Mike sat back, arms folded, not entirely convinced. When David finished, Sandra asked, "Are these talks live, or are they done via Zoom?"

Mike replied, "They're live. We get business owners and tenants in a room, give them free coffee and biscuits, and then I do my pitch."

Sandra nodded. "Okay, here's what I want you to do. Change the beginning of your presentation. Start by asking the audience, 'If you believe global warming is a problem for our future, please raise your hand.' You raise your hand first, encouraging them to follow. Then, look around the room and point out how the majority of people believe global warming is an issue. Next, ask them, 'Raise your hand if you don't want your children growing up in a world where clean drinking water isn't guaranteed.' Again, you raise your hand and draw attention to those who follow. Continue with another question, like, 'Do you want your children to grow up in a world without water wars, where sustainable energy is the norm?' Get them to raise their hands again."

Sandra continued, "By now, you'll have most people with their hands up. You've got them agreeing on something fundamental. You've used the principle of consistency. People like to remain consistent with what they've previously agreed to, especially in front of others. Then, you segue into your usual pitch. Remind them subtly throughout that they all agreed they don't want their children growing up in a world ravaged by global warming and environmental decline. This will make your call to action far more powerful. You're not just asking them to buy green lighting; you're asking them to stay consistent with the values they just publicly supported."

Mike was sceptical but intrigued. He decided to give Sandra's strategy a shot. At his next presentation, he made the changes. He felt awkward at first, raising his hand and prompting the audience to do the same. But as he looked around the room and saw the hands go up, something shifted. He could see it in their eyes. They were more engaged. When he moved into his usual pitch, it was as if he wasn't just talking at them—they were listening, really listening.

By the end of the meeting, he'd closed his first sale. Then another. And another. It was like a dam had broken. Over the following weeks, as he continued using Sandra's approach, his conversion rate skyrocketed. It got to the point where, at some meetings, half the audience had already converted from previous sessions. Mike would even ask, "If you've already made the switch to greener lighting, raise your hand." And hands would go up, prompting others to join in, not wanting to be left out.

The results were astounding. The very people who'd seemed so resistant just weeks before were now enthusiastic participants in the council's green initiative. Mike went back to the council office with a triumphant grin. "Sandra," he said, "you're a genius. I thought your idea was a bit out there, but it's worked wonders. Consistency, who knew?"

Sandra smiled and replied, "It's all about understanding people, Mike. They want to do the right thing; sometimes they just need a little nudge in the right direction."

Mike had learned an invaluable lesson in psychology that day. He realised it wasn't just about the numbers or the product; it was about making people feel like they were part of something bigger, something important. And in the end, that made all the difference.

Lesson: Sometimes, it's not about the product or the numbers—it's about tapping into people's values and beliefs. By using the principle of consistency, Mike learned how to connect with his audience on a deeper level, getting them to commit to their own publicly stated values. When people feel they are part of a greater cause and see their actions as consistent with their beliefs, they are far more likely to engage and make a change. The right psychological approach can transform a tough sell into an easy win.

Chapter Seven

Make Them Like You

Make Them Like You

Peter Harding had been a life insurance salesman for nearly a decade. Every morning, he'd wake up, put on his slightly faded navy suit, grab his briefcase, and head out for another day of door-to-door sales. The streets of his suburban patch were well-worn under his feet. Most doors had opened to him at least once, and many had been politely — or not-so-politely — closed in his face. Business had been slow lately, and Peter was feeling the pinch. His commissions were drying up, and he needed a win.

One crisp Tuesday morning, Peter found himself on a quiet, tree-lined street he'd visited many times before. He approached the first house of the day, a modest brick home with a freshly painted door. Taking a deep breath, he knocked. After a few moments, the door creaked open to reveal an elderly woman with a kind face, her grey hair pulled back in a neat bun.

"Good morning, ma'am," Peter began with a warm smile. "I'm Peter Harding from National Life Insurance. I was wondering if you might have a few minutes to chat about some great new policies we have—"

The woman interrupted him gently. "I'm afraid I'm not interested, young man. Thank you."

Before he could get another word out, the door was closed, leaving Peter standing there, feeling the familiar sting of rejection. He sighed and moved on to the next house, then the next. Each knock felt heavier than the last, each rejection adding weight to his shoulders. By midday, he had nothing to show for his efforts but a series of polite refusals and a growing sense of frustration.

As Peter trudged down the pavement, he spotted a small café on the corner and decided to take a break. He ordered a cup of coffee and sat by the window, watching the world go by. He couldn't help but over-hear a conversation at the next table. A young woman was enthusiastically chatting with a group of friends about a book she'd recently read on psychology.

"It's all about how people make decisions," she ex-plained. "There's this principle called 'liking.' People are more likely to say yes to someone they like. It's fascinating!"

Peter's ears perked up. He thought about his ap-proach. For years, he had stuck to the script, focus-ing solely on the product — the benefits, the premi-ums, the small print. He realised he'd been neglecting something crucial: the human element.

Determined to turn things around, Peter gulped down the rest of his coffee and headed back out. He decided to try something different. The next house he approached was a quaint, blue cottage with a white picket fence. He noticed a small garden filled with colourful flowers. As he knocked on the door, he felt a new sense of purpose.

The door opened, and a middle-aged man in a plaid shirt appeared, a hint of caution in his eyes.

"Good afternoon, sir!" Peter greeted him with a broad smile. "I couldn't help but admire your beautiful garden. Those roses are absolutely stunning."

The man's face softened. "Thank you! I've been working on them for years. It's my little passion project."

Peter nodded, genuinely interested. "I can tell. They're fantastic. My wife's been trying to get our garden to look half as good as yours, but we've still got a long way to go."

The man chuckled, and Peter could see the tension ease. "It takes time and patience, but it's worth it," the man replied. "I'm Jack, by the way."

"Nice to meet you, Jack. I'm Peter Harding. I'm with National Life Insurance, but I promise I'm not here to give you the hard sell. I'm more interested in hearing about those roses, to be honest."

Jack smiled, and for the next few minutes, they chatted about gardening. Peter listened intently, nodding along, occasionally sharing a light-hearted joke or story. He felt the connection growing, the rapport building.

Finally, Peter gently steered the conversation. "You know, Jack, just like you've put so much care into your garden, I believe in helping people protect what they've worked so hard for. I'd love to chat with you about some options that might suit your needs if you're open to it."

Jack looked thoughtful but not dismissive. "I usually don't go for insurance salesmen, but you're alright, Peter. Let's sit down and talk."

Over the next hour, Peter used what he'd learned from the café conversation. He established his credibility by clearly explaining the policies, tailored his pitch to Jack's needs, and most importantly, he listened. He asked questions about Jack's life, his concerns, and what he wanted for his family. By the end of their discussion, Jack wasn't just a potential customer; he felt like a friend.

Jack agreed to a policy that suited his situation, and Peter left with a signed contract in his briefcase and a renewed sense of purpose in his heart.

As Peter continued his rounds that afternoon, he found himself more at ease. He focused on making genuine connections, finding common ground, and showing empathy. He noticed the difference almost immediately. Doors were opening, conversations were happening, and by the end of the day, Peter had not one but three new clients.

That evening, as he walked home under the setting sun, Peter couldn't help but smile. He realised that the secret to sales wasn't just about having the best pitch or the most knowledge. It was about being liked — about building real, human connections.

Peter never looked at sales the same way again. He knew now that the power of liking wasn't just a psychological principle; it was a way of life, a way of treating people with respect, kindness, and genuine interest. And in a world where so many doors were closed, he had found the key to opening them.

Lesson: Sales isn't just about the product; it's about the person. Peter Harding discovered that people are more likely to buy from someone they like and trust. By focusing on building genuine connections and showing a sincere interest in his potential clients, he transformed his approach and found success where there had only been rejection. The power of liking isn't just a sales tactic—it's a fundamental human principle. Treat people with kindness and authenticity, and you'll find doors opening that were once closed.

Chapter Eight

Put It In A Picture

Put It In A Picture

C hris Walker was a force to be reckoned with—a black belt in Karate and a respected teacher who had spent years working alongside the police, teaching them self-defence techniques. He was a master at his craft, a man whose movements were as fluid as water and as powerful as a storm. Yet, despite his martial prowess, he was facing a battle of a different kind—filling his Karate studio with new students.

His dojo was his pride and joy, a place where he could pass on his knowledge and passion for martial arts to the next generation. But lately, the dojo had been emptying out. The sound of bare feet shuffling across the mats had become less frequent, the yells of enthusiastic children practising their katas had grown faint, and the steady income from membership fees was drying up.

Chris knew he had to do something. The rent for the studio wasn't going to pay itself, and his savings were quickly dwindling. He had a problem on his hands—a big one.

Determined to turn things around, Chris decided to take matters into his own hands. He was convinced that if he could just speak to enough people, he could convince them of the value of learning Karate. After all, it was a discipline that had taught him so much—focus, self-control, strength. Surely, he could make others see this too.

He started by going door-to-door around his neighbourhood. He'd knock, wait for someone to answer, and then begin his pitch.

"Hi there! My name is Chris, and I run a Karate dojo just a few blocks away. I'm here to offer you or your children a chance to learn self-defence and gain confidence. Would you be interested in joining our beginner classes?"

Most people were polite but dismissive.

"Oh, we're not interested, thank you."

"Sorry, we're busy."

"No, we don't have time for that."

Rejection after rejection, Chris's confidence began to wane. He was used to physical challenges, but this was different. This was personal. He was passionate about Karate, and it hurt to see that others didn't share his enthusiasm.

After a particularly gruelling day of door-knocking and not a single sign-up to show for it, Chris sat down on a park bench, feeling defeated. Sweat dripped down his face, not from physical exertion but from the crushing weight of rejection. What was he doing wrong? How could he make people see the value of what he was offering?

That's when he noticed a young woman sitting across from him, watching a series of videos on her phone. She seemed engrossed, smiling and nodding as if the person on the screen was speaking directly to her.

Chris couldn't help but be curious. What was so captivating? He caught a glimpse of the screen—it was a motivational speaker, talking about how to improve sales by understanding the psychology of decision-making. The words "framing effect" flashed across the screen. Intrigued, Chris jotted down the term and decided to look it up when he got home.

Back in his small apartment, Chris began to dive deep into the concept of framing. He learned that the way information is presented—the 'frame'—can significantly influence people's decisions. He realised he had been focusing too much on the features of his classes—the techniques, the discipline, the exercise. But what about the benefits? What about the things people truly cared about?

He learned about different framing techniques:

Emphasising Benefits Over Features: Instead of talking about Karate itself, focus on what it could do for the students—confidence, safety, fitness.

Loss Aversion: People are more motivated to avoid losses than to gain something. What if he framed Karate as a way to avoid losing their sense of safety or missing out on personal growth?

Contrast Effect: Show the stark difference between living with fear or insecurity versus living with confidence and strength.

Chris felt a spark ignite inside him. He had been approaching this all wrong. It wasn't about Karate; it was about what Karate could do for them.

The next day, armed with his newfound knowledge, Chris decided to try a different approach. He designed a simple flyer with a bold headline:

"Are You Prepared to Defend Yourself and Your Family? Don't Wait Until It's Too Late."

He included some stark statistics about local crime rates—how many muggings or assaults occurred within a few miles of their neighbourhood. Then, beneath that, he listed the benefits of learning Karate:

Gain Confidence: Never feel helpless or scared again.

Get Fit and Strong: A fun way to stay in shape.

Protect Yourself and Loved Ones: Learn life-saving skills.

And finally, at the bottom, he added: "Join our dojo today and get the first month free. Don't miss out on this limited-time offer!"

He also decided to employ a bit of anchoring. He wrote that the regular price for classes was £100 a month but, for a limited time, new members could join for just £50. This made the offer seem like an even greater deal.

Chris went out again, this time with a different mindset. He wasn't just selling Karate classes; he was offering peace of mind, fitness, and confidence. He started by visiting local shops and community centres, placing his flyers on bulletin boards, and leaving stacks at the counters with a friendly word to the staff.

Within days, he began to notice a change. The phone started ringing. People were calling, curious about the self-defence classes. They were not just interested in learning Karate—they were interested in feeling safer, more confident, and fitter. Chris noticed that when he emphasised what they stood to lose—like their safety or peace of mind—people were more eager to listen.

He hosted a free demonstration class at the local community centre, framing it as a chance to learn "how not to be a victim". The room was packed. Chris used the contrast effect to his advantage, showing how simple techniques could make a difference between being helpless and being prepared. He spoke in simple terms, using positive framing to show what life could be like with the skills they would learn.

By the end of the session, many of the attendees signed up on the spot, not wanting to miss out on the limited-time offer. Chris's dojo began to fill up again, and within a few weeks, it was thriving. The sound of feet shuffling across mats, the sharp snaps of punches and kicks, and the loud, enthusiastic shouts filled the air once more.

Chris had won his battle—not by sheer force, but by reframing the fight. He learned that sometimes, it's not about what you're selling, but how you present it.

And that's how Chris transformed his struggling Karate studio into a flourishing dojo, simply by understanding the power of framing.

Lesson: The way you frame your offer can make all the difference. Whether it's in sales, marketing, or everyday communication, framing helps you emphasise benefits, appeal to emotions, and guide decision-making. Always think about what your audience truly cares about and how you can present your message in a way that resonates with them.

Chapter Nine

It Can Stop A Ship

It Can Stop A Ship

Sebastian leaned back in his leather chair, the view of the London skyline stretching out behind him. His gallery, a luxurious haven for art collectors, was bustling with whispers of intrigue and desire. Today, he had an important appointment—a new client, Mr. Harold Kensington, a hedge fund manager with a penchant for exclusive pieces. Sebastian knew this sale would require all his finesse and understanding of human psychology. Kensington wasn't just any buyer; he was a wealthy man, used to getting what he wanted, but also wary of being taken for a ride.

Sebastian specialised in selling one-of-a-kind or few-of-a-kind art pieces to the rich and famous. He had a reputation for making even the most sceptical buyers see the value in his offerings. Today, his weapon of choice would be the art of anchoring.

The bell on the gallery door chimed, announcing Kensington's arrival. Sebastian rose to greet him, a warm smile on his face.

"Mr. Kensington, a pleasure to finally meet you in person," Sebastian said, extending his hand. "I've handpicked a few pieces that I believe will capture your unique taste."

Kensington smiled politely. "Thank you, Sebastian. I've heard a lot about your gallery. I'm curious to see what you have in store."

As they strolled through the gallery, Sebastian stopped in front of a large canvas—a striking abstract by a contemporary artist. He didn't dive straight into the price. Instead, he began with a story.

"This piece," Sebastian began, "is reminiscent of one we sold just a few weeks ago to a rather famous collector. You might have heard of him—Michael

Jackson? He was particularly taken by the artist's unique approach to colour and form. That painting went for £1.2 million."

Kensington's eyes widened slightly, his interest piqued. "Really? £1.2 million, you say?"

Sebastian nodded. "Indeed. And at a recent auction, another work from the same artist fetched close to £1 million. Quite the statement piece, wouldn't you agree?"

By now, Sebastian had laid the groundwork. The anchor was set. Kensington, whether he realised it or not, was now judging the value of the painting in front of him against the prices of similar works recently sold. The figure of £1.2 million floated in his mind, not just as a price, but as a standard of value.

Kensington studied the painting, a thoughtful expression on his face. "It is striking, I'll give you that. What's the asking price for this one?"

Sebastian paused, as if considering. "For you, Mr. Kensington, I'm prepared to offer it at a special price—£950,000. Considering its provenance and the recent sales, it's quite a competitive offer."

Kensington hesitated, the gears in his mind turning. The initial price points—£1.2 million, £1 million—were already influencing his perception of value. £950,000 suddenly seemed like a bargain.

"But," Kensington began, "is it really worth that much? The market can be so unpredictable."

Sebastian leaned in, his voice soft, almost conspiratorial. "Art, Mr. Kensington, is not just about market trends. It's about passion, about making a statement. And owning a piece like this... well, it's not just a purchase. It's an investment in cultural legacy."

He could see the doubt flicker and then fade from Kensington's eyes. Sebastian continued, using another technique from his anchoring arsenal—the contrast effect.

"Let me show you another piece," he said, guiding Kensington to a smaller, less impressive painting. "This one, while beautiful in its own right, is listed at £600,000. A good piece, certainly, but compared to the other..." He let the sentence trail off, allowing Kensington to fill in the blanks.

Kensington looked between the two paintings. The second one, though still high in price, didn't hold the same allure after being compared with the more expensive piece and its compelling story. The initial £1.2 million anchor had done its job. The first painting, with its rich backstory and the price comparison, seemed like the better deal.

"I see what you mean," Kensington finally said, his voice more assured. "I do like the idea of owning something with such a story behind it. Let's go with the first piece."

Sebastian smiled. "An excellent choice, Mr. Kensington. I'll have the paperwork drawn up immediately."

As they wrapped up the sale, Sebastian reflected on the power of anchoring. By setting a high anchor with the mention of Michael Jackson's purchase and a recent auction, he'd shaped Kensington's perception of value. The £950,000 asking price felt more reasonable, almost like a discount, when compared to the initial figures he'd mentioned.

For Kensington, this was more than a transaction; it was a journey into the world of art, filled with passion, prestige, and a touch of exclusivity. For Sebastian, it was another day in the life of an art dealer who knew how to make his clients see value—real or perceived.

As Kensington left the gallery, Sebastian turned back to the vast collection of art that filled the room. Another satisfied client, another successful sale. He knew the principles of anchoring would guide his next negotiation, his next story. After all, in the world of high-end art, perception was everything—and he was the master of it.

Lesson: Anchoring is a powerful sales technique that sets a reference point to influence a buyer's perception of value. By strategically introducing high price points early in the conversation, a salesperson can make their offer seem more appealing and reasonable. This method works especially well in high-stakes environments, like luxury art sales, where perceived value can sway decisions. When used effectively, anchoring not only guides the buyer's judgement but also enhances the appeal of the product, leading to successful sales.

Chapter Ten

Compare Apples With Oranges

Compare Apples With Oranges

S ue sat in her office, staring at the quarterly sales report. It was the same story as last quarter—and the one before that. Their CRM, a sophisticated tool packed with all the features a small or medium-sized business could need, was well-regarded. But when it came to getting customers to move from the £99 basic plan to the £299 premium plan, they were hitting a wall.

The £299 package was objectively better. It offered advanced analytics, customisable dashboards, and enhanced customer support. It should have been an easy sell. But customers weren't biting. They didn't see the value in upgrading, especially at three times the price of the basic package. Sue and her team had tried everything to shift perception. They'd hosted webinars, created side-by-side comparison charts, and even offered limited-time discounts. But none of it seemed to make a significant dent.

With only 15% of their users on the £299 plan, revenue growth was stagnating. Worse, Sue's team was spending hours on one-on-one calls trying to convince potential upgrades. The constant grind was wearing everyone down, and Sue knew they couldn't keep this up forever.

"We need something drastic," Sue said during a team meeting. "We're losing momentum. We're stuck pushing a product customers don't seem to want."

Lucy, her most seasoned sales rep, chimed in. "It's not that they don't want it. They just don't see the point in paying three times as much. We're not showing them why they need it."

Sue nodded, feeling the weight of the challenge. She knew they needed a fresh perspective. Someone who could see beyond the current setup and provide a new angle. That's when she decided to call Tom.

Tom was a sales consultant known for his unconventional approaches to sales strategy. He was the kind of guy who thrived on flipping the script. Sue reached out, and after an enthusiastic conversation, Tom agreed to take on the challenge.

He spent a few days immersing himself in the company's pricing structure, talking to the sales team, and even getting feedback from customers.

When he finally returned with his findings, he had a gleam in his eye. "You don't need to add anything more to your product," Tom said. "You need to take something away."

The room went silent. Take something away? They had already streamlined their offerings to focus on the essentials. What else could they possibly strip back?

Sue looked perplexed. "What do you mean, Tom? We've tried positioning the value, we've tried adding extras, but none of it has worked. What are we missing?"

Tom leaned forward, a smile playing at the corner of his mouth. "Your problem isn't the £299 package itself. It's how it looks compared to the £99 package. Right now, customers see two choices: £99 or £299. And in their minds, they're thinking, 'Why pay more when the £99 does enough?'"

He paused, letting his words hang in the air for a moment.

"So, what do we do?" Lucy asked, her curiosity piqued.

"We use the Contrast Principle," Tom replied. "We're going to introduce a third option. A new middle-tier plan priced at £299, but with fewer features than the current £299 plan. Then, we're going to raise the price of the existing £299 package to £999. But here's the kicker—we'll offer the £999 package at a permanent discount to £299."

Sue frowned, trying to wrap her head around the idea. "So, you're suggesting we create a new £299 package that's worse than the one we already have, and then increase the price of our current £299 plan to £999, but with a permanent discount back to £299?"

Tom nodded. "Exactly. It's all about perception. We're anchoring their expectations. When customers see the £999 price slashed to £299, it suddenly looks like they're getting an incredible deal. The middle-tier £299 package, which is less than half as good as the discounted £999 package, will make the £299 offer seem irresistible."

Sue decided to trust Tom's expertise and gave the go-ahead. They worked quickly to restructure the pricing tiers:

Basic Plan: £99 a month, with limited features.

Middle Plan: £299 a month, with some additional features but less than the original £299 package.

Premium Plan: Originally priced at £999 a month, but permanently discounted to £299. This was essentially the original £299 plan, but now positioned as a premium, top-tier option.

The website was updated, marketing materials revised, and the sales team trained on the new approach. The launch was subtle but intentional. The team held their breath, wondering if this bold move would work.

To everyone's surprise, the impact was almost immediate.

Within a week, calls started pouring in. Customers were no longer comparing the £99 plan to the £299 plan. Instead, they were fixated on the "incredible value" of the £999 package being offered for only £299. Suddenly, the old objection of "why pay three times as much?" disappeared. Now, it was "how can we not grab this deal while it's available?"

The perception of savings was powerful. Customers felt they were getting something exceptional for a bargain. The new middle-tier plan, priced the same as the discounted premium, only served to make the £299 "special offer" appear even more valuable.

The contrast was stark, and it worked brilliantly.

By the end of the month, the shift was undeniable. The number of customers on the £299 "special offer" plan doubled. Customers who had been content with the £99 plan saw the new pricing structure and thought, "Why settle for less when I can get more for the same price as the middle-tier?"

The feedback from customers was overwhelmingly positive. They felt they were getting premium features at a bargain price. And the sales team was reinvigorated. For the first time in months, they weren't fighting an uphill battle. They were closing deals with ease, enthusiasm returning to their voices.

Sue couldn't believe it. The solution wasn't about adding more value or cutting prices. It was about how they positioned the product. By creating a new, less appealing middle-tier option and then contrasting it with a discounted premium, they had changed the way customers perceived the value.

She looked over at Tom, who was leaning casually against the wall, watching the team with a satisfied smile. "I have to hand it to you, Tom," she said. "You've pulled off a miracle."

Tom chuckled. "It's no miracle. Just understanding human nature. People don't make decisions in a vacuum. They need something to compare. We gave them a frame of reference, and the choice became obvious."

Sue nodded, understanding now. It wasn't about the price itself. It was about how the price was framed—using the Contrast Principle to create a sense of value, urgency, and desire.

In the weeks that followed, the company continued to see an uptick in premium plan sign-ups. Revenue was climbing, and the energy in the office was palpable. Sue felt a wave of relief. They'd cracked the code, not by changing the product but by changing the perception.

And just like that, with a simple shift in strategy, Sue had turned a seemingly unsolvable problem into a powerful selling point.

The lesson was clear: in sales, it's not always about what you sell, but how you sell it. And sometimes, the best way to make something more appealing is simply to change what you compare it against.

Lesson: The power of the Contrast Principle had transformed the way Sue's customers viewed her product. It wasn't just about adding value but framing it in a way that made the choice clear and compelling. A small change in strategy, a big change in results.

Chapter Eleven

The Phone In The Door Technique

The Phone In The Door Technique

Mike, a seasoned sales and marketing director at a fast-growing technology company, stared at his phone, his frustration mounting with each passing second. He had spent the past two weeks cold calling local businesses to pitch their new service, "Ring Fence Marketing." The service was innovative, targeting every possible search term within a 50-square-mile radius of a business, instead of focusing on the high-traffic keywords that every SEO agency was already promising to rank.

But there was a problem. Nobody was listening. His calls were met with a series of abrupt rejections, polite brush-offs, or worse—being hung up on mid-sentence. Mike knew that the problem wasn't the service. Ring Fence Marketing was a game-changer for local businesses, offering them exclusivity and a wider reach. The issue lay in getting the business owners to understand the value before they decided they weren't interested.

Mike was starting to lose faith. The phone sat heavily in his hand, as if mocking him. What was he doing wrong? Why couldn't he even get a foot in the door?

Then it hit him. The answer was in the problem itself. He needed to get his foot in the door—literally. His old sales training came flooding back to him. The "Foot-in-the-Door" technique, a classic approach in sales and persuasion, could be his way out of this slump.

Instead of diving headfirst into the full pitch about Ring Fence Marketing, he needed a smaller ask. Something easy for the business owners to agree to, something that wouldn't make them immediately think, "Oh great, another salesperson trying to sell me something I don't need."

With a newfound sense of purpose, Mike formulated his plan. He wouldn't start with a sales pitch. He would begin with a question—a small, harmless request that would get his prospects engaged and thinking.

The next morning, Mike was back at his desk, ready to give his new approach a try. He took a deep breath and dialled the number of a local solicitor's office in Manchester.

"Good morning, this is Mike from Contact Funnels. I hope I'm not catching you at a bad time?"

There was a brief pause, followed by a wary, "No, what is this regarding?"

Mike knew this was his moment. "I was wondering if I could ask you a quick question about your online marketing strategy? Just a minute of your time."

The voice on the other end softened slightly. "I suppose. Go ahead."

Mike smiled. The first step had been taken. "Do you currently use an SEO agency to handle your digital marketing?"

"Yes, we do," came the reply.

"Great! I'm curious, do you find that your agency is also working with other solicitors in the same area? Like, say, a competitor down the road?"

There was a pause. "Actually, yes, I think they are. But that's normal, isn't it?"

"Absolutely, it's very common," Mike agreed. "But have you ever wondered if that might be a conflict of interest? I mean, if your SEO agency is helping your competitor rank for the same keywords, does that really benefit you?"

The silence on the other end told Mike he had struck a chord. The solicitor hesitated, "I hadn't really thought about it that way."

"Exactly!" Mike said, his voice upbeat but not pushy. "That's precisely why I wanted to speak with you today. At Contact Funnels, we've developed a different approach. We call it Ring Fence Marketing, and it's designed to give businesses like yours a real edge over the competition by targeting 100% of the search traffic within a 50-square-mile radius. No competing interests, no shared keywords with your competitors. Just pure, focused marketing to help you stand out."

The solicitor was listening now. Really listening. "That sounds interesting, but how does it actually work?"

Mike knew he had them. "That's a great question. Would you mind if I sent you a brief overview? It's a simple one-page document that explains exactly how Ring Fence Marketing works and how it could help you dominate your local area."

"Sure, I'd like to see that," came the response, more enthusiastic now.

"Fantastic! I'll get that over to you right away. And if you have any questions after you've had a chance to review it, I'd be more than happy to go over it in more detail."

As he hung up, Mike felt a surge of triumph. He hadn't made a sale—not yet—but he had done something just as valuable: he had gotten his foot in the door. By starting with a small, easy request and building from there, he had turned a cold call into a warm lead.

Over the next few days, Mike refined his approach, making more calls and focusing on asking that first, small question. He found that more often than not, once business owners started thinking about the potential conflict of interest with their current SEO agencies, they were more than willing to hear him out.

He wasn't pitching them the moon; he was guiding them step-by-step, from a small commitment to a larger one, each time building on their desire to be consistent with their previous actions.

Soon enough, Mike wasn't just getting his foot in the door—he was being invited inside, metaphorically speaking. Business owners were genuinely interested in learning more about Ring Fence Marketing, and the sales began to roll in.

By using the Foot-in-the-Door technique, Mike turned his cold calls into opportunities, and opportunities into sales. He learned a valuable lesson: sometimes, all it takes to change the course of a conversation—and a career—is the power of that first, small step.

And from that day forward, whenever Mike picked up the phone, he knew exactly how to start.

Lesson: The Foot-in-the-Door technique isn't about making a sale right away. It's about making a connection, building trust, and setting the stage for the real conversation. Just like Mike, all it takes is one small step to begin a journey that leads to success.

Chapter Twelve

The Door In The Face

The Door In The Face

Matt sat in the sleek, glass-walled conference room of his father's company, nervously tapping his fingers on the polished table. He had one last chance to prove himself, one final opportunity to close a deal that had eluded him for months. His father's words echoed in his mind, "If you can't sell this business for 90 million, I'll have to bring someone else in." Matt knew he couldn't afford to fail again—not this time.

His father had never been one to hand out praise or rewards easily. Every success Matt had ever tasted had been hard-earned, and this deal was no different. The prospective buyers—a group of high-powered executives from China—were due to arrive any minute. Matt knew they were tough negotiators. They would be looking to get the best deal possible, and so far, none of the other offers had even come close to the 90 million mark his father wanted.

Matt wasn't just fighting for his commission. He was fighting for his future. If he could pull this off, he'd earn a 1% commission, enough to finally launch his own venture, a business of his own that he'd been dreaming about for years. But if he failed? He'd have to start from scratch, with nothing but his father's disappointment and another black mark on his record.

He took a deep breath and straightened his tie. He needed a strategy—a way to turn the odds in his favour.

As the Chinese executives entered the room, Matt could feel his heartbeat quicken. They moved with a quiet confidence, their expressions giving nothing away. He greeted them warmly, trying to mask his anxiety. "Welcome, gentlemen. I'm Matt, and I'll be taking you through the presentation today."

He launched into his pitch, presenting the company's strengths with passion and precision. He highlighted the untapped potential, the strategic advantages, the lucrative growth opportunities. He knew the company was worth every penny of the 90 million asking price, but convincing these seasoned executives was a different matter.

Matt could see them nodding, but there was no spark of excitement, no indication they were ready to commit. He pushed on, adding more data, more compelling reasons to buy. But then, as he wrapped up, Mr. Li, the lead negotiator, leaned back in his chair and said calmly, "Thank you, Matt. It's a strong case, but 90 million is more than we're willing to pay. We're prepared to offer 70 million."

Matt's heart sank. 70 million was even lower than the other offers they'd received. He could feel the frustration rising, his dreams of independence slipping away. But then, an idea began to form in his mind. He remembered a strategy he had once read about—the Door-in-the-Face Technique. It was a bold move, but if he played it right, it could work.

Matt leaned forward, his eyes meeting Mr. Li's with a calm confidence. "I appreciate your offer, Mr. Li, but 70 million is far too low. In fact, I was going to suggest a price much higher than 90 million."

The executives exchanged surprised glances. Matt continued, "We're looking at 130 million, considering the exclusive opportunities and the strategic position this acquisition offers your company in the European market."

There was a moment of stunned silence. Mr. Li raised an eyebrow, clearly taken aback. "130 million? That's significantly more than your original asking price. How do you justify such a figure?"

Matt had anticipated this reaction. He smiled slightly and said, "I understand it's a big number, but it reflects the full scope of what you'd be acquiring—not just a company, but a gateway into new markets, new technologies, and future partnerships."

He paused, letting the words settle in. "However," he continued, "I recognise that's a significant commitment. So, I'm willing to consider a more reasonable figure. What if we discussed 95 million? It's closer to your range and still reflects the true value of the company."

Matt watched as Mr. Li and his team huddled together, speaking in hushed tones. He could feel the tension in the room, but he knew he had them thinking. He had planted the seed of doubt, making them wonder if 70 million was far too low.

After a few moments, Mr. Li straightened up and looked directly at Matt. "95 million is still more than we initially wanted, but we can see the value in your offer. You've made a compelling case."

Matt felt a wave of relief wash over him, but he maintained his composure. He wasn't done yet. "I'm glad to hear that, Mr. Li. How about we settle at 90 million? It's a fair compromise, and it ensures both parties leave satisfied. You get a valuable company, and we get a fair return on our investment."

There was a pause as Mr. Li considered the proposal. Finally, he nodded. "90 million it is. We have a deal."

Matt could hardly believe it. He had done it. Not only had he secured the sale at the price his father demanded, but he had also managed to do it in a way that made the buyers feel they were getting a fair deal. By starting with an exaggerated figure and then scaling back, he had used the Door-in-the-Face Technique perfectly, creating a sense of relief and fairness.

The executives shook hands with Matt, and he could see a slight smile on Mr. Li's face. "You're a good negotiator, Matt. We look forward to working with you."

As they left the room, Matt allowed himself a moment to breathe. He had proven himself today. Not just to his father, but to himself. He had shown he could handle the pressure, make the right decisions, and close the deal. More than that, he had shown that he had what it takes to succeed on his own terms.

Lesson: The Door-in-the-Face Technique wasn't just about making unreasonable demands; it was about setting the stage for a win-win outcome. By starting high and then offering a more reasonable alternative, Matt had managed to turn a potentially disastrous situation into a triumph. He had learned a valuable lesson: in sales, it's not just about what you ask for—it's about how you ask for it. Today, he had asked the right way, and now his future was brighter because of it.

Chapter Thirteen

Scarcity Of Opportunity

Scarcity Of Opportunity

Sebastian Smith, a man whose name echoed in the boardrooms of the largest companies in the world, sat in his office at FocusSoft. The office was sleek, modern, and minimal, a reflection of the man himself. At sixty, Sebastian was still sharp as ever. He had been the top-earning CEO in the UK for five years straight, a remarkable feat for someone who, by all accounts, was getting close to retirement.

As he gazed out the window overlooking the city, he couldn't help but wonder what was next. The idea of spending his golden years golfing or fishing held no appeal. Instead, Sebastian had a vision—a way to pass down his decades of knowledge. He would offer one-on-one coaching to three lucky managing directors or CEOs of smaller companies. But this wouldn't be a typical coaching service. For £25,000 a month, Sebastian would meet once a week for an hour with each client and share everything he knew—everything that had made him the success he was.

There was just one problem: no one knew about it.

Enter Daniel, a bright-eyed, eager marketing guy Sebastian had taken on. "Leave it with me," Daniel had said. "I'll start marketing this straight away."

And he did. Daniel launched an email campaign to every managing director and CEO in the UK. He set up paid ads on every social media platform you could think of—Facebook, Google, LinkedIn. He even ran targeted ads in business magazines. He followed every tactic he had learned in his career. Three months later, they had...nothing. Not a single booking.

Sebastian called Daniel into his office. "So, Daniel, how many spots have we filled?" Sebastian asked, expecting some good news.

Daniel shifted uncomfortably in his seat, his face a mixture of frustration and defeat. "None. Not a single one."

Sebastian raised an eyebrow. "None? After three months?"

Daniel sighed. "I've done everything—email campaigns, social ads, paid search. I even tried influencer marketing. Nothing's worked. Honestly, I think it's the price. £25,000 is a lot, and there are other coaches out there charging way less, offering more time with their clients. I just don't think this is something people want at this price."

Sebastian chuckled and leaned back in his chair. "Daniel, £25,000 is pocket change for these companies. They probably spend more than that on coffee every month. The problem isn't the price—it's the way you're selling it."

Daniel looked confused. "But I've used every trick in the book."

Sebastian stood up and walked to the window. "That's the problem. You've been marketing this like a small business would. We're not selling a gym membership or a low-cost service. We're offering something rare—something no one else can get. Do you know how many CEOs would kill for the chance to sit down with someone like me and learn everything I know? The problem isn't the offer—it's how you've positioned it."

Sebastian turned to his PA, Cynthia, who had been quietly sitting in the corner, scribbling notes. Cynthia was in her 50s, a bit overweight, and always looked slightly frazzled, but she was brilliant at her job.

"Cynthia," Sebastian said, "get in touch with every major newspaper, business journal, and podcast you can find. Tell them that the UK's highest-paid CEO is offering his time to three companies. Only three. Tell them this is a once-in-a-lifetime opportunity, and once these spots are gone, they're gone for good. Make sure they understand how unique this is."

Cynthia nodded, already jotting down her plan.

"Daniel," Sebastian continued, turning back to the young marketer, "it's not about the price. It's about scarcity. I'm not offering this to just anyone. I'm offering it to three companies, and those three companies will be the only ones who ever get access to my knowledge. That's what makes it valuable."

Daniel sat there, wide-eyed, as Sebastian's words sank in. It was a different kind of sales pitch, one that didn't rely on flashy ads or endless email campaigns. It was about making the opportunity feel rare—exclusive.

Cynthia wasted no time. She worked day and night, calling every journalist, every business podcaster, and every news outlet she could find. She pitched the story relentlessly, even when most weren't interested. But persistence paid off. Slowly but surely, the story gained traction.

Within a week, the buzz was undeniable. Headlines read: "UK's Highest Paid CEO Offers Rare Coaching Opportunity to Just Three Lucky Companies". Business podcasts were talking about it. Even those who had no interest in coaching were intrigued by the rarity of the offer.

Soon enough, Cynthia's phone was ringing off the hook. Companies were desperate to be one of the three. Some even offered to pay more than the £25,000 just to secure a spot. In less than a week, all three spots were filled, and there was a waiting list of companies willing to pay double, even triple, to get the chance to work with Sebastian.

Daniel watched in awe as Sebastian's simple strategy—highlighting the scarcity of the opportunity—created an avalanche of interest. It wasn't about marketing tricks. It wasn't about lowering the price. It was about making people realise they were about to miss out on something they could never get again.

Sebastian smiled as he sat down with his first client. The principle of scarcity had done all the heavy lifting.

Lesson: sometimes, it's not about what you're offering—it's how rare and valuable you make it seem. Scarcity can turn an offer into something irresistible, even at a premium price.

Chapter Fourteen

Quick Quick Quick

Quick Quick Quick

S arah sat at her cluttered desk, staring at the spreadsheet on her laptop. The numbers didn't lie. Sales for the upcoming music event were dismal. Out of the thousand seats available, only 320 tickets had been sold. She could already imagine the half-empty venue, the awkward silence between songs, and the disappointed faces of the band members. She knew the stakes. If she couldn't sell the tickets, it would be a disaster—not just for the band but for her reputation as an events organiser.

Her stomach twisted in knots at the thought of failure. The event was just two weeks away, and she had run out of ideas. She had tried everything—social media ads, flyers, even a radio interview. Nothing worked. The truth was, the band wasn't well-known, and there wasn't much buzz about the event. It was meant to be a breakthrough gig for them, but at this rate, it might just break them altogether. Sarah felt the weight of their dreams on her shoulders. If she couldn't pull this off, it wouldn't just be her who'd be out of a job—the band's career might be over before it even began.

"Think, Sarah, think!" she muttered to herself, tapping her pen against her notepad. She knew she needed to do something drastic to spark interest and get people to buy tickets, but what?

She glanced at the clock. 4 p.m. She had less than two weeks to turn this around. Panic started to creep in, and she could feel her heartbeat quicken. She took a deep breath and decided to call Tom, a mentor who had been in the event business for over two decades. If anyone could help her, it was him.

"Hey, Tom, it's Sarah," she said when he picked up. "I'm in a bit of a pickle. I've got this music event, and I just can't sell the tickets. I've tried everything. Do you have any ideas?"

Tom paused for a moment. "Have you tried creating urgency?"

"Urgency?" Sarah repeated, confused.

"Yes, urgency. People act when they feel they might miss out on something. You've got to make them feel like they need to be there, or they'll regret it. There are lots of ways to do this—time-sensitive offers, limited stock announcements, upcoming price hikes. You need to make them feel like if they don't act now, they'll lose out."

Sarah listened intently. She had heard about the principle of urgency before but had never considered it in this context. She felt a spark of hope.

"Okay, but how do I do that?" she asked.

Tom chuckled. "Well, for starters, how about a limited-time discount? Offer a 20% discount on tickets for the next 48 hours. Announce it everywhere—social media, emails, even on your event page. Make it clear that it's only for 48 hours. People love a bargain, and the ticking clock will push them to buy."

Sarah quickly jotted down notes. "That's a great idea, Tom. What else?"

"You could also try a countdown timer on the event page, showing how many tickets are left. If people see the numbers dwindling, they'll act fast. And, you can play on the exclusivity angle—mention that only the first 100 buyers get VIP access or something special."

Sarah's mind raced with possibilities. She thanked Tom and hung up, feeling a surge of energy. She had a plan.

That evening, Sarah sprang into action. She updated the event page, adding a countdown timer showing the end of the 48-hour discount period. She sent out an email blast with a bold headline: "48-Hour Flash Sale! 20% Off Tickets—Don't Miss Out!" She made sure to mention that only a limited number of tickets were available at this discounted rate. She crafted social media posts with a sense of urgency, using phrases like "Act Now!" and "Last Chance!" She even asked the band members to share the posts with their followers, adding their own messages about how special the event was going to be.

She watched as the discount countdown ticked away on the event page. An hour passed, then two. Nothing. Her heart sank a little. What if it didn't work? What if she had misunderstood Tom's advice? But then, just before she was about to call it a night, she saw the first notification pop up on her phone—Ticket Sale Confirmed.

Then another. And another.

Within the first six hours, they sold 150 tickets. Sarah's phone kept buzzing through the night with notifications. She stayed up late, watching the numbers climb, her heart racing with excitement. The next morning, the discount period still had 24 hours to go, and they had already sold over 300 more tickets. She couldn't believe it.

By the end of the 48-hour sale, nearly 600 tickets had been sold. The venue was more than halfway full, and there was still a week to go. Sarah decided to keep up the momentum. She set up a second count-down—this time announcing that only 200 tickets remained before they reached full capacity. She sent another round of emails and social media posts, emphasising the limited availability.

It worked like a charm. The fear of missing out was real, and people scrambled to secure their tickets. Within days, they had sold out. Sarah couldn't believe it. She had done it. She had turned a potential disaster into a sold-out event.

On the night of the event, the venue was packed. The band played their hearts out, feeding off the energy of the enthusiastic crowd. Sarah watched from the back, a satisfied smile on her face. She had not only saved the event, but she had also learned a valuable lesson: creating urgency can drive people to act. She knew she would use this strategy again.

As the band played their final song, Sarah's phone buzzed once more. It was a text from Tom: "Congrats on the sell-out, Sarah. You did it. Remember, urgency works wonders. Don't forget it."

Sarah smiled. She wouldn't forget. Not now. Not ever.

Lesson: Creating a sense of urgency can dramatically increase sales and drive customer action. By implementing tactics such as limited-time discounts, countdown timers, and highlighting limited availability, Sarah was able to transform a failing event into a sold-out success. The urgency compelled potential customers to act quickly, showcasing the effectiveness of urgency as a powerful sales strategy. When people feel they might miss out on something valuable, they're more likely to make a purchase. Remember, urgency motivates action.

Chapter Fifteen

Once Upon A Time

Once Upon A Time

Arthur Greenwood, a well-known author from the southwest coast of the UK, had a voice that could make any tale sound like a bedtime story. With his farmer's accent and the ease of a man who had lived a life full of stories, he could spin a yarn that would make you lean in closer, eyes wide, and your mind painting pictures with every word. Arthur was not just a writer; he was a storyteller, a master of weaving words into experiences that would stick with you long after you heard them.

Now, Arthur had a car. Not just any car, mind you, but a classic. A gleaming, pristine beauty that he'd owned since the 1960s. It was a sight to behold, all curves and chrome, with the kind of vintage flair that turned heads wherever it went. To the untrained eye, it was worth maybe £20,000 or £30,000 at most. But Arthur wanted to sell it for £150,000. A steep price, you might think. A price for fools. But Arthur knew better. He knew the power of a story.

In a few days, an interested party was coming to see the car, and Arthur had a plan. He wasn't just going to show them a car; he was going to sell them a piece of history, a piece of magic. He was going to make them feel the worth of that car in their bones.

The day arrived, and a sleek, black sedan pulled up outside Arthur's cottage. Out stepped a well-dressed man, probably in his mid-40s, with an air of sophistication and a look that said he had more than a little bit of money to spare. Perfect.

"Good afternoon," Arthur greeted him with a warm, toothy grin, his accent thick and inviting. "Ye must be Martin. Come on in, lad. I've got just the thing to show ye."

Martin nodded, extending a polite handshake, and followed Arthur around to the side of the house where the car was kept under a large, protective cover. Arthur paused for a moment, letting the suspense build before slowly pulling back the cover, revealing the car in all its glory.

"Oh, it's a beauty," Martin said, eyebrows raising in genuine admiration.

"Aye," Arthur nodded, "But she's not just a beauty. She's a legend."

Martin looked at him, curiosity piqued. "A legend, you say?"

Arthur chuckled softly, nodding. "Oh, aye. Ye see, this car's more than just metal and paint. This here's a story on four wheels. Would ye like to hear it?"

Martin couldn't help but smile. "Go on then."

Arthur took a deep breath and began. "It was the summer of 1969, not long after I'd gotten me hands on her. She was brand new then, fresh out the factory. I took her up to Scotland, to the highlands, for a bit of a race. It was me against a local lad, a bit of a legend himself back then. We raced through the moors, the wind whipping through our hair, engines roaring like a pair of angry lions. It was neck and neck for miles. But this lass here," he patted the car fondly, "she had something special. She had heart. And she won. First race out, and she won."

Martin listened, eyes locked on Arthur, drawn into the story. He could almost see it — the winding roads, the green hills, the thrill of the chase.

Arthur continued, "That was just the start. Over the years, she's raced in all sorts of places — the cliffs of Dover, the back roads of Cornwall, even the streets of Monaco. And she didn't just race; she won hearts. She carried a young man to his first love. She was there when I wrote my first bestseller, parked outside the publisher's office. Every ding on her, every scratch, it tells a story. She's been driven by the likes of Sir Sterling Moss — yes, the Sterling Moss — and even once had James Bond himself, Sean Connery, take the wheel for a charity drive."

Martin's mouth had fallen open slightly, his mind reeling with the imagery. "Sean Connery? Really?"

"Aye, really," Arthur said, smiling. "And let me tell ye, lad, when ye sit in this car, ye don't just drive; ye become part of that story. Ye feel the thrill, the adventure, the history coursing through ye. It's not just about where she's been; it's about where she'll take ye. Imagine the stories ye can tell. Imagine the looks on yer friends' faces when ye tell 'em you're driving a car with a pedigree like this."

Arthur leaned in a bit closer, lowering his voice to a near whisper, making it all the more captivating. "This isn't just a car. It's a legacy. And legacies, they don't come cheap. They're worth every penny, every pound, because they're not just bought; they're earned."

Martin nodded, swallowing hard. He could feel his heart racing, his mind already spinning tales of his own. He could see himself behind the wheel, could hear the roar of the engine, could imagine the awed looks on his friends' faces as he told them the stories, Arthur's stories. But now, they'd be his stories too.

"So, Martin," Arthur said, his voice warm and inviting, "are ye ready to become part of this car's next chapter?"

Martin didn't hesitate. "Absolutely. Where do I sign?"

And just like that, Arthur had done it. He hadn't sold a car. He'd sold a story, a feeling, a dream. And he'd done it for £150,000.

The power of storytelling in sales was clear. When you make them feel the story, they're not just buying a product; they're buying a part of that story. And stories, real stories, they're priceless.

Lesson: Storytelling transforms a sales pitch into an emotional journey. By weaving a compelling narrative around a product, you engage the buyer's imagination and emotions, making them see value beyond the price. Sell the story, not just the item, and the buyer will see themselves in it.

Chapter Sixteen

Inch Wide, Mile Deep

Inch Wide, Mile Deep

Danny, a fifty-something veteran of the training industry, sat in his small, cluttered home office, staring at his computer screen. He had finally decided to leave the company he had worked for his entire career, where he spent 40 hours a week teaching the same course over and over. Fed up with the monotony, he was determined to break free and start his own venture. He was confident he could make a fortune selling his courses.

Danny spent weeks meticulously crafting his content. He poured years of knowledge and experience into his courses, covering every aspect of his field. He was convinced that his expertise would naturally attract customers, and he imagined himself becoming a millionaire, earning far more than he ever did working for someone else. But the reality was a harsh wake-up call.

When Danny launched his courses, sales trickled in at a dismal pace. Days turned into weeks, and weeks into months. Despite his best efforts, he couldn't seem to sell more than a few copies. Danny was baffled. He knew his material was good, and he had decades of experience to back it up. Why weren't people buying?

Danny became desperate. He tried everything—Google Ads, Facebook marketing, webinars. He even lowered his prices, hoping to attract more customers. But nothing worked. He watched as other platforms sold courses for as little as £15, £20, or at most £150. Meanwhile, his own courses, priced at £3,000, gathered digital dust.

He couldn't understand it. How could his courses, packed with valuable content, fail to sell while cheaper, less comprehensive ones thrived? Frustration gnawed at him. He felt like he was back at square one, but this time without the security of a steady job. His savings were dwindling, and the dream of striking out on his own was rapidly turning into a nightmare.

Everywhere he looked, there were cheap courses on generic topics—general sales techniques, broad marketing strategies, and the like. But Danny wanted to offer something different. He wanted to charge a premium, believing his detailed, all-encompassing courses were worth the price. But it became clear that the market didn't see it that way.

One evening, over a cup of lukewarm coffee, Danny stumbled upon a podcast by a successful online entrepreneur. The speaker, an expert in niche marketing, was talking about something Danny had never considered: the concept of "inch wide, mile deep." It was all about specialising in a very narrow niche and offering something so tailored, so specific, that the right audience would pay a premium for it.

Danny realised he had been making a critical mistake. He had been trying to sell his courses to everyone, but in doing so, he appealed to no one. His courses were too broad, too generic. They didn't speak directly to any particular customer or solve a specific problem uniquely. The entrepreneur's words echoed in his mind: "People will pay more for something that feels like it was made just for them."

Inspired, Danny went back to the drawing board. He took a hard look at his courses and started to rethink his strategy. What if, instead of trying to be everything to everyone, he focused on being the absolute best in one tiny area? What if he created a course specifically for sales managers in the tech industry, or marketing strategies tailored exclusively for dental practices?

He decided to test this new approach. Danny developed a course that was hyper-focused on sales techniques for small, family-owned bakeries—a niche market he knew had unique challenges. He reached out directly to bakery owners, speaking their language, understanding their pain points, and offering solutions tailored to their specific needs.

This time, the response was different. The bakery owners were intrigued. They felt like Danny understood them, that his course was speaking directly to their unique situation. Slowly but surely, sales started to pick up. His new niche courses were priced higher, but they offered something the cheaper, generic ones didn't—specialisation.

Within months, Danny was finally seeing the success he had dreamed of. His bank account, once dwindling, began to grow. He had found his "inch wide, mile deep" niche, and it made all the difference.

Danny's story is a powerful lesson in the importance of specialisation. By focusing on a specific, narrow niche and offering something uniquely valuable to that audience, he transformed his business from a struggling start-up to a profitable venture. In the end, it wasn't about the quantity of his courses, but the quality and relevance to the right people.

Lesson: Don't try to be everything to everyone. Find your niche, understand it deeply, and become the best in that space. That's where true success lies.

Chapter Seventeen

Speak To Your Customers

Speak To Your Customers

Marcus sat at his kitchen table, head in his hands, staring at the untouched cup of coffee in front of him. His eyes were tired, dark circles forming under them, a result of another sleepless night. His wife, Sarah, sat across from him, equally exhausted. Their three children had been up half the night, but it was their youngest, Emma, who had caused the most chaos. At six years old, Emma was a beautiful little girl with big, expressive eyes, but she had severe autism.

Loud noises, bright lights, and busy environments sent her into an uncontrollable spiral.

Just yesterday, they had tried to take her to the local park. Within minutes of arriving, the clatter of other children playing, the dogs barking, and the general hum of a busy Saturday morning overwhelmed her. Emma had screamed, clutched her ears, and ran in frantic circles, terrified. Marcus and Sarah had tried everything they could to calm her, but it was no use. They'd left in a hurry, feeling defeated, embarrassed, and utterly helpless.

"I can't keep doing this," Marcus muttered to himself. "There must be something out there, something better than these useless headphones." He glanced over at the bulky, overpriced noise-cancelling headphones sitting on the counter. They were meant to help Emma, but she hated them. They were uncomfortable, ineffective, and they only muffled the noise, never truly blocking it out.

The frustration gnawed at Marcus. As a father, it was his job to protect his daughter, to keep her safe and calm, but every outing turned into a disaster. The looks from strangers, the whispered comments, and the judgement weighed on him. He couldn't even take his daughter to the park or the grocery store without fearing a meltdown. The anxiety of anticipating Emma's next episode was like a constant hum in his mind.

"What are we supposed to do?" Sarah asked, her voice breaking. "We can't keep her locked up at home. But every time we go somewhere, it's like we're playing Russian roulette. We never know when she's going to explode."

Marcus knew she was right. They had to find a solution, not just for their sanity, but for Emma's well-being. She deserved to experience life without fear, without the overwhelming assault of noise that seemed to be everywhere.

He spent hours searching online, reading articles, joining forums, and talking to other parents. But nothing seemed to fit. Then one evening, while browsing a late-night forum, he stumbled upon an idea that lit a spark in his mind. What if there was a portable, instant, quiet space that could be set up anywhere? A place where Emma could escape the chaos, even in the noisiest environments?

The idea consumed Marcus. He spent days sketching designs, working on prototypes, and testing different materials. He knew it had to be lightweight, portable, and easy to set up. Something that could be carried in a handbag and popped open in seconds. It also needed to be effective, truly blocking out the external noise and creating a safe, quiet space for Emma.

His first few attempts were rough—flimsy frames that collapsed, fabrics that didn't block enough sound, zippers that jammed. But he kept refining, kept testing. He was driven by the thought of Emma finally being able to enjoy a day out without the fear of an impending meltdown. Finally, after months of work, he had something that he was proud of—a foldable, noise-cancelling panel that created an instant quiet space.

He called it QuietSpace.

The product was simple but revolutionary. It was small enough to fit in a purse, and it could be set up in under a minute. The fabric was specially designed to absorb and block out noise, creating a silent sanctuary amidst the chaos of the outside world. Marcus knew he had something special, but now he needed to get the word out. He needed a value proposition that would speak directly to parents like him, those who lived in constant fear of loud, noisy environments.

Marcus sat down with his notepad and began to write. He knew that the value proposition had to be clear, direct, and centred around the needs of parents with autistic children. It had to convey the unique benefits of QuietSpace and differentiate it from the ineffective headphones and other noise-cancelling products on the market.

"Find Your Focus, Anywhere."

This was his main slogan. It captured the essence of what QuietSpace offered—a portable, instant quiet environment that allowed children like Emma to find calm and focus, no matter where they were. It was concise, memorable, and spoke directly to the needs of parents who wanted their children to have a safe, quiet space.

"A Silent Sanctuary in a Noisy World."

This value proposition emphasised the unique ability of QuietSpace to provide an escape from the chaos of everyday life. For parents with autistic children, this was a game-changer. It wasn't just about reducing noise; it was about creating a personal sanctuary where their child could feel safe and calm.

"No More Panic, Just Peace."

Marcus knew that many parents, like him, dreaded taking their children out in public because of the fear of a meltdown. This value proposition tapped into that fear, offering QuietSpace as the solution. It wasn't just a product; it was peace of mind.

"Transform Loud Places into Quiet Spaces."

This statement highlighted the transformative nature of QuietSpace. It wasn't just a panel—it was a tool that could turn any environment, no matter how loud or chaotic, into a quiet, calming space for a child with autism.

Marcus tested these propositions with a small group of parents, including those he'd met in the online forums. The feedback was overwhelmingly positive. Parents loved the simplicity and clarity of the messages. They could immediately see the benefit of QuietSpace, not just as a product, but as a life-changing solution for their families.

The next time they went to the park, Marcus felt a familiar knot of anxiety in his stomach. But this time, he wasn't worried about Emma having a meltdown. He had QuietSpace with him. As soon as Emma began to show signs of distress, Marcus popped open the QuietSpace panel. Emma stepped inside, and within moments, she was calm, her panic fading away.

Parents watched in awe as Marcus closed the panel around Emma, creating an instant, quiet sanctuary amidst the noisy park. There were no screams, no frantic running—just peace.

For the first time in a long time, Marcus felt a sense of relief wash over him. He had found a solution, not just for Emma, but for every parent who had ever felt the fear and frustration he had. QuietSpace was more than just a product. It was a lifeline.

Lesson: The power of a strong value proposition lies in its ability to speak directly to the customer's needs and concerns. By focusing on the unique benefits of QuietSpace and addressing the specific problems faced by parents with autistic children, Marcus created a compelling, customer-centric message that resonated deeply with his target audience.

Chapter Eighteen

FOMO

FOMO

Mark had been in the tent business for 15 long years. Summers were a frenzy. Families across the country prepared for their camping holidays, rushing to buy the perfect tent. His shop was always buzzing during these months, with tents flying off the shelves. But, as vibrant as the summers were, the winters were equally bleak. Sales dried up completely, and Mark found himself fighting to keep his business afloat. Year after year, it was the same cycle: sell enough in the summer to scrape through the winter.

His competitors were no different. Every tent supplier in town followed the same strategy. They all counted on the summer rush and resigned themselves to barren winters. Mark often saw his rivals posting on social media about their struggles during the cold months, lamenting over empty stores and unused stock. They had all accepted this pattern. Tents didn't sell in winter, and that was the end of it. Or was it?

Mark's situation had become desperate. He had enough tents in storage to last the next five years, but the cost of storing them was eating away at his profits. The banks wouldn't lend him more money—he was already in debt up to his eyeballs. If he didn't figure out a way to sell some of his stock this winter, he might have to close his shop for good. The thought of going out of business gnawed at him day and night.

One particularly cold evening, as Mark sat in his dimly lit shop, he noticed an email notification pop up on his laptop. It was a marketing newsletter, the kind he usually deleted without reading. But today, he was desperate for ideas, so he opened it. The subject line read: "Harnessing FOMO to Boost Your Sales."

FOMO—Fear of Missing Out. Mark knew about it, of course. It was the idea that people are often driven by the fear of missing out on something rather than the prospect of gaining something. He'd seen it work wonders in other industries, but tents? He wasn't so sure.

Then it hit him. Why not create a sense of urgency, a fear of missing out? He could turn his misfortune into a unique selling point. The more he thought about it, the more it made sense. What if he convinced customers that this was their last chance to buy one of his high-quality tents? He could emphasise that once they were gone, they were gone forever.

He decided to take a risk. The next morning, he began drafting a bold new campaign. It was unlike anything he'd done before. The headline was striking: "Final Clearance Sale – Last Chance to Own the Best Tent on the Market!" He added phrases like "limited stock," "never available again," and "once in a lifetime offer." He wanted to make it crystal clear: if you don't act now, you'll lose your chance to get a top-quality tent at a bargain price.

Mark also highlighted the benefits his tents offered: durable materials, easy setup, weather resistance. He painted a vivid picture for his potential customers. He showed families enjoying their camping trips, happy and secure in one of his sturdy tents. But he also stirred a bit of fear—what if they waited until summer and the tents were all gone? What if they missed out on the chance to grab the perfect tent at an unbeatable price?

He launched his campaign online, across social media, and even put up signs around town. The initial response was slow. Days went by, and Mark started doubting his idea. Maybe everyone was right. Maybe tents just didn't sell in the winter. But then, a week into the campaign, something changed. A customer came in, then another, and another. One woman told Mark she'd seen his ad and didn't want to miss out. She'd been planning to buy a tent for her family's summer trip anyway, so why not now, when the deal was so good?

Word spread, and soon, Mark's shop was bustling again. Customers were calling in to ask about the sale.

Some even drove hours just to get their hands on one of his tents. Mark couldn't believe it. For the first time in 15 years, he was selling tents in the winter. Not just a few—dozens. He watched in amazement as his stock dwindled, his storage room clearing out faster than he'd ever imagined.

By the time spring rolled around, Mark was in a much better financial position than he had been in years. His gamble had paid off. He not only survived the winter but thrived. His competitors were stunned. Many of them had continued to sit on their stock, believing there was no market for tents in the colder months. But Mark had proved them wrong. He'd tapped into a psychological principle that was as old as time: people are more motivated by the fear of losing something than the desire to gain something.

Mark had turned the tables by using loss aversion to his advantage. He'd shown his customers what they stood to lose by not acting, rather than what they could gain. And it worked. He had created a sense of urgency, a fear of missing out, that pushed people to buy when they otherwise wouldn't have considered it.

From then on, Mark looked at every off-season with a fresh perspective. He wasn't just another tent seller competing in a crowded market. He was a savvy businessman who knew how to make psychological principles work for him. And as he looked around at his now thriving business, he realised that sometimes, the biggest rewards come from taking the biggest risks.

Lesson: People are more likely to act from the fear of missing out than they are from the potential for gain.

Chapter Nineteen

Social Scarcity

Social Scarcity

Malcolm was a man of action. He had built his business from the ground up, driving from one auction house to another, hunting for bargains. He had a knack for spotting what would sell and what wouldn't. Over the years, he'd stocked his warehouse with all sorts of goods, from antique furniture to modern gadgets. But today, as he walked through the aisles of his warehouse, he was on a mission.

He was tired of seeing the same old footstools stacked in the corner, gathering dust. He had bought them at an auction about five years ago, and they had been a hot seller at first. Back then, he had put a 50% off tag on them, claiming it was a special, limited-time offer, and they flew off the shelves. He'd managed to sell most of them that way. But these last 25… they just wouldn't shift.

"These have been sitting here too long," Malcolm muttered to himself, tapping his foot impatiently. He needed the space for new stock, and he needed it fast. "Right, time to clear these out for good."

Malcolm knew about the power of scarcity. He had used it many times to great effect. People hated missing out; the fear of losing something forever was a strong motivator. So he devised a plan. He'd put up a big, bold message on the website: "Only 25 left! Last chance to buy! When they're gone, they're gone!" He fired off an email to his customer list, highlighting the urgency of the situation. He even added a countdown timer for good measure, ticking away with each passing second.

But the response was underwhelming. Orders trickled in slowly. Two days went by, and only three footstools were sold. Malcolm couldn't believe it. He had used this technique so many times before. Why wasn't it working now?

Perplexed, Malcolm spent the next few hours combing through the website analytics. Traffic was there; people were clicking through to the product page, but they weren't buying. Frustrated, he decided to take a break and go home. Maybe he was missing something obvious.

That evening, over dinner, Malcolm couldn't help but unload his woes onto his wife, Lisa. She was always his sounding board, his voice of reason.

"I don't get it," he said, pushing his food around his plate. "I've created urgency. I've told them these are the last ones. I even set a countdown timer! Why isn't anyone buying?"

Lisa, ever the patient listener, nodded. "How many of these did you sell in the past?" she asked.

Malcolm pulled out his phone and checked. "We sold 155 of these, easy. And people loved them back then."

"Alright," she said thoughtfully. "And what did those customers say about them?"

He scrolled through some old emails and found the reviews. There were dozens, maybe even a hundred. Glowing testimonials, customers raving about how the footstools were a bargain, how stylish they looked in their kitchens and living rooms, even how well they had held up over the years. There were even pictures of the footstools in people's homes, looking perfect.

Lisa smiled. "There's your answer. People want to know that others have bought them and love them. It's not just about scarcity. It's about seeing that others think it's a good deal too. Scarcity is good, but on its own, it can feel a bit... desperate. Add some social proof, and it gives it credibility."

Malcolm nodded slowly, understanding dawning on him. He had been so focused on creating urgency that he had forgotten to show potential customers why these footstools were worth buying in the first place.

The next day, Malcolm was back in the office early. He updated the website. This time, under the "Only 22 Left! Last Chance to Buy!" banner, he added a carousel of customer photos, each one showing the footstools in a beautifully decorated home. Beneath the photos, he included snippets of the best reviews:

"An absolute bargain at £150!" "Couldn't believe the quality for the price!" "These look fantastic in my kitchen – everyone asks where I got them!"

He made sure the testimonials were front and centre, right under the scarcity message. Then, he sent out another email blast, this time highlighting the reviews and photos, letting people see for themselves that these footstools were not just limited in number but also loved by many.

The response was immediate. Within hours, the orders started flooding in. The combination of scarcity and social proof worked like magic. By the end of the day, all 22 remaining footstools were sold out. Malcolm couldn't believe the difference it made.

He leaned back in his chair, a satisfied smile spreading across his face. He'd learned an important lesson: it wasn't just about creating urgency. People needed reassurance. They needed to know that they were making the right choice, especially when time was running out.

Scarcity with social proof wasn't just a tactic; it was a powerful strategy. One that, when used correctly, could turn even the most stubborn of stock into a sell-out success.

Lesson: Sometimes when they're struggling to sell something, the best salespeople combine sales strategies and really hammer home the sales

Chapter Twenty

Target Everybody Hit Nobody

Target Everybody Hit Nobody

A lex sat in his cramped office, the hum of computers filling the air. It was late in the afternoon, and he had already gone through his third cup of coffee. His company, Insightlytics, had seemed so promising just a few months ago—a cutting-edge data analytics tool that could transform how businesses visualised their data. He had envisioned companies lining up to buy his product, but reality had turned out very different.

Despite the flashy launch and endless hours of coding, sales were dismal. Alex had attended countless startup events, spoken at networking meetups, and posted endlessly on LinkedIn and Twitter. He'd even sent personal emails to CEOs, hoping someone would see the value in his product. But the responses were lukewarm at best.

The worst part? His competitors were closing deals with the very companies he'd targeted. He couldn't understand it. His product had features that were light-years ahead of theirs, but no one seemed to care. Every time he opened his sales dashboard, it was like a punch to the gut—barely any leads, and fewer still converted to paying clients.

As the months passed, the pressure mounted. Investors started raising eyebrows and asking tough questions. Alex felt like a fraud, pretending everything was fine when deep down, he knew it wasn't. He was burning through his company's cash reserves, and with each day, his runway shortened. At night, when the city went quiet, Alex would lie in bed staring at the ceiling, wondering if he had made the biggest mistake of his life. The dream he'd worked so hard for felt like it was slipping through his fingers.

"Maybe I'm not cut out for this," he thought to himself one night after yet another fruitless meeting.

Desperate and exhausted, Alex reached out to Sarah, his mentor. Sarah was a no-nonsense entrepreneur who had successfully built and sold multiple tech startups. She had seen it all, from product launches that flopped to miraculous turnarounds. If anyone could help, it was her.

They met at a small coffee shop just outside the city. Alex poured out his frustrations as Sarah listened intently, not interrupting. When he finally stopped talking, Sarah leaned back in her chair and took a sip of her coffee.

"Alex," she said, "you're trying to do everything, and that's why nothing is working."

Alex frowned. "What do you mean?"

"Your product is brilliant. I've seen it. But you're too scattered. You're marketing to everyone, hoping something will stick, but that's not how sales work—especially in tech. You need to focus."

Sarah's words stung, but he knew she was right. He'd been casting his net too wide, trying to sell Insightlytics to any business that would listen, regardless of whether they truly needed his product or not.

"You need to narrow your focus," Sarah continued. "Find a niche where your software solves a specific problem, and sell directly to them. Right now, your pitch is too broad. Let me ask you this—who needs real-time data analytics the most?"

Alex thought for a moment. "I suppose small e-commerce businesses could use it to track customer behaviour in real time. They need to know what's selling and what isn't. But I've been targeting large corporations with bigger budgets."

Sarah smiled. "Exactly. You're chasing the big fish, but they already have tools in place, or they're too slow to adopt something new. These small e-commerce businesses? They're nimble, they need to move fast, and they could use your product to stay competitive."

Sarah didn't stop there. She also pointed out that Alex's product demo was far too complicated. Potential customers were getting lost in all the technical details when they really just wanted to know how Insightlytics could make their lives easier.

"You're overwhelming them," Sarah said. "Simplify your pitch. Show them the one thing that will matter to them—how your software will save them time and money. Focus on that, and you'll see results."

Alex left the meeting with a clear plan: narrow his focus to small e-commerce businesses and simplify his demo to show how Insightlytics could increase their sales and customer engagement. But Sarah had one more piece of advice before he left.

"You also need to stop doing everything yourself," she said. "Hire a small sales team, even just one or two people who understand this niche and can build relationships while you focus on product development."

It felt like a revelation. Alex had been so focused on his product that he forgot he couldn't wear every hat in the company. He needed help.

Over the next few weeks, Alex threw himself into revamping Insightlytics' marketing strategy. He rewrote the website, making sure every word spoke directly to small e-commerce business owners. He replaced his complicated demo with a short, user-friendly video that showed, in simple terms, how his product could help them track customer behaviour and increase sales.

With Sarah's guidance, Alex also hired a sales manager, Jessica, who had years of experience in the e-commerce sector. Jessica knew exactly how to speak the language of small business owners, and within weeks, they began seeing the results.

Leads started pouring in. Alex couldn't believe how much of a difference it made when he focused on a specific market. E-commerce businesses were not only interested in Insightlytics—they were excited. They saw how the product could help them grow, and they were willing to invest.

By the end of the quarter, Alex had closed several significant deals. The company's revenue was growing, and for the first time in months, Alex felt like he could breathe again.

As Insightlytics continued to gain traction, Alex realised something important: having the best product didn't matter if no one understood its value. What mattered was the right strategy—finding the right market, speaking their language, and delivering a solution to their specific problem.

His startup had made it through the storm, and Alex learned the power of narrowing his focus. It wasn't just about sales—it was about survival.

Lesson: When starting out in business, success comes from identifying a specific niche that genuinely needs your product and can afford it. Target them directly, speak their language, and solve their specific problem.

By focusing on a smaller, defined market, you avoid the trap of trying to appeal to everyone. Instead, you tailor your message, refine your product to meet their exact needs, and build trust. When you're starting out, being a big fish in a small pond is much more effective than being lost in the ocean.

Chapter
Twenty-One

Reverse The Risk

Reverse The Risk

S teve had a knack for turning struggling businesses into wildly successful ventures. He'd spent
years perfecting his methods, crafting a course that, in
his eyes, was a golden ticket for any business owner
who followed it. His course promised to double the
size of a business within six months—no matter the
industry. But there was a catch, and it wasn't with the
course itself. The problem was that Steve's industry
was tainted. The "Make Money Online" crowd was
saturated with frauds and con artists, selling over-

priced snake oil that never worked. The market was jaded. Nobody trusted the promises anymore.

Steve launched his course full of excitement, convinced that people would see it for what it was—genuine, transformative, and reliable. But it didn't take long before his optimism turned to frustration. No matter how much he shouted about how good his course was, no one was buying. He couldn't understand it. He knew his product was solid, yet people were ignoring it. They were clicking on his ads, visiting his website, even reaching the payment page—but then abandoning their carts.

Confused and frustrated, Steve sought help from a mentor. The mentor listened to his frustrations, nodding as Steve ranted about how unfair it was that his course wasn't selling.

"Here's the problem," the mentor said. "It's not the product, mate. It's the fact that people don't believe you. They've been burned too many times before. The risk is too high for them to take a chance on you."

Steve nodded, but that wasn't enough for him. "But my product works," he said. "How can I make them believe that?"

"You need to reverse the risk," the mentor suggested. "Offer a guarantee—something that shifts the risk from them to you."

So Steve went away, worked up a "no-questions-asked" 90-day money-back guarantee, and plastered it all over his website. He expected the sales to start rolling in, but the results were underwhelming. Sure, he sold a few courses—three in total—but nowhere near the numbers he had hoped for. Once again, Steve felt like he was on the verge of giving up.

He went back to his mentor. "I tried the guarantee," Steve said, "and I sold a few more, but it's not working like I thought it would."

"Alright," the mentor said, "what about social proof? Have you got testimonials from your previous clients?"

Steve thought about it and realised he had never asked. So, he went to his past clients and asked for testimonials. Some of them sent glowing reviews, and Steve posted them on his site.

Again, the results were better—but still sluggish. Sales trickled in, but it wasn't the flood Steve needed. He was getting traffic, people were looking, but they weren't biting. It felt like something was still missing.

Frustrated, Steve returned to his mentor, feeling like he'd tried everything. "What else can I do? I've given a guarantee, I've got testimonials, and still, it's not enough."

The mentor leaned back and smiled. "Right. Let's do something radical. You've got a solid product, right? But the industry you're in—it's filled with scams. People have been burned over and over again, and even your guarantee isn't enough to overcome their fear. So, we're going to reverse the risk completely."

Steve's ears perked up. "How?"

"We're going to make it so attractive that the customer has no reason to say no. You're going to tell them that if they don't double their business in 90 days, not only will you give them their money back, but you'll pay them double what they invested. And, on top of that, you'll give them a checklist to follow—a roadmap. As long as they can prove they followed the steps, they'll either succeed or get paid for trying."

Steve blinked. "You want me to pay double if they fail?"

"Yes," the mentor said firmly. "This isn't just about a guarantee anymore. It's about showing that you believe in your product so much, you're willing to pay them if it doesn't work. That's complete risk reversal. The risk isn't on them at all anymore. It's on you."

It felt like a massive gamble, but Steve knew he had nothing to lose. His sales were stagnant, and this was his shot at making a real difference. So, he reworked his sales page. Now, it offered the "Double Your Investment Back" guarantee, with the clear checklist that guided buyers through the exact steps they needed to take.

Within days of relaunching, Steve noticed the difference. Sales started pouring in, far more than before. The promise of being paid if the course didn't work attracted people who had previously been too scared to trust anyone. And as they followed the roadmap, many of them succeeded. His testimonials multiplied, and word-of-mouth spread like wildfire. Steve's product quickly became one of the best-selling courses in its niche.

In the end, it wasn't the product that had been the issue. It was the customer's fear of risk. Once Steve took that fear away—once he put the risk squarely on his own shoulders—the floodgates opened. The "double money-back" offer made people feel secure, and it also showed that Steve believed in his product enough to back it with his own money.

The lesson? If you want people to buy from you, you've got to remove the obstacles in their minds. People don't want to feel like they're gambling with their money. By reversing the risk, you make it easy for them to say "yes."

And that's how Steve went from struggling to sell to being one of the most successful entrepreneurs in his field. All it took was flipping the risk and showing people they had nothing to lose.

Lesson: Shift the perceived risk onto your shoulders and turn the purchase into a partnership, not a solo gamble for your customer.

People don't want to feel like they're taking a risk alone. By sharing the burden, you show them you're invested in their success too. It's not just about selling a product—it's about building trust and making your customer feel supported every step of the way. When you stand behind your offer and take on some of the risk, you turn the buying process into a mutual commitment, making it easier for the customer to say "yes."

Chapter Twenty-Two

The Power Of Personal Stories

The Power Of Personal Stories

Mike sat at his desk, staring at the sales figures on his computer screen. They weren't bad, but they weren't great either. He had a game-changing product, the Magic Page Plugin, designed to revolutionise how local businesses marketed themselves online. Yet, despite its undeniable potential, sales were stagnant. He couldn't understand why. After all, this tool had the power to transform any local business into a dominant player in their region, just as it had done for his locksmith company in Manchester.

The Magic Page Plugin wasn't just another mass-page-building tool. It was crafted with precision, built specifically for local businesses, and optimised to target locations within a set radius. In theory, this should have been enough to make sales fly off the shelf. But it wasn't happening. Mike's presentations were thorough. He'd go into detail about the product, explaining its features, how it worked, and why it was superior to the competition. But the response was lukewarm.

One afternoon, frustrated and at his wits' end, Mike rang his friend Tim, a seasoned sales expert from South Carolina. Tim had been in sales for years and knew the ups and downs of the business. After venting his frustrations for a while, Mike finally asked, "Why aren't people buying this? It's the best thing out there for local businesses, but they just don't seem to care!"

Tim chuckled softly on the other end. "Mike, people don't buy products. They buy you."

"What do you mean?" Mike asked, confused.

"They need to feel a connection. They need to know you understand their problems, that you've been where they are, and most importantly, that you've used this product to solve your own problems. You need to tell them your story."

Mike frowned. "But I've been explaining why the product is great."

"That's not enough," Tim said firmly. "You've got a personal story behind this product, don't you? Share that. Let them see how it changed your life. People want to know the person behind the product, not just the features. They want to see that you've been in their shoes and that this product is the solution."

Mike paused, thinking back to his early days as a locksmith in Manchester. He remembered the struggle—the days when he ranked number one for "locksmith Manchester" but still wasn't getting enough calls. He remembered discovering that website covering every tiny village around Manchester, renting it, and watching his phone blow up with calls. It was the turning point that had transformed his business. But he had never shared that with anyone when selling the Magic Page Plugin.

Maybe Tim was right. Maybe it was time to be more open.

The next time Mike had a meeting with a potential client, he did something different. He sat down, and instead of diving into the technical details of the Magic Page Plugin, he started talking about himself. He told the client how, as a young locksmith, he had struggled to get enough work, even when his website ranked number one. He explained how he stumbled upon a local website that targeted every small town in a five-mile radius around Manchester. Once he'd put his phone number on that site, the calls hadn't stopped.

Mike shared how he had painstakingly built similar sites for other towns, manually creating hundreds of location-specific pages. It had taken weeks, but the results had been worth it—his locksmith business exploded. Then he explained how that experience led him to create the Magic Page Plugin, a tool that could now do in minutes what had once taken him weeks.

The client sat up, intrigued. For the first time, Mike saw real interest in their eyes. By the end of the meeting, the client signed up on the spot.

Mike was stunned. He called Tim straight after. "It worked," he said, amazed. "I told them my story, and they bought!"

Tim laughed. "I told you, mate. People want to connect with you. The product will sell itself if they believe in you."

From that moment on, Mike made his personal story the centrepiece of every sales pitch. He talked about his struggles, his failures, and his eventual breakthrough. He shared how the Magic Page Plugin wasn't just a product he created—it was the result of years of hard work, trial and error, and real-world experience. And just like that, sales started rolling in.

The more Mike shared his story, the more people connected with him, and the more they believed in the product. Over time, the Magic Page Plugin became the number one tool for local businesses looking to dominate their online market. Mike didn't need to chase customers anymore—they came to him.

Lesson: personal stories matter. By sharing his own journey, Mike had turned a struggling product into a market leader. He realised that when people feel a connection, when they see themselves in your story, they're far more likely to trust you—and trust leads to sales.

And that, as Mike learned, was the real magic behind his success.

Note from the author: This is the first time in this book that I've provided a specific framework, and that's because it works exceptionally well. I've used this approach successfully for many years, and I'm confident that sharing personal stories with this structure will significantly boost your sales and conversions.

Framework: Here's how Mike structures his personal stories when sharing them with potential clients:

I wanted to achieve this – Start by identifying the goal or desire that aligns with what the client wants to achieve.

I tried doing this – Explain the initial steps you took, which mirrors what the client might be doing now (status quo).

I failed because of this – Highlight the reason for failure, focusing on the common obstacles that clients also face.

I thought all hope was lost – Acknowledge the frustration and pain of not getting the desired results.

I was about ready to give up – Emphasise the growing pain and how close you were to quitting.

I discovered this – Introduce the turning point or solution (the discovery of your product or method), either through your own efforts or with someone's help.

I tried doing this – Share how you applied the new method (your discovery or product) and the changes made.

I achieved success – Reveal the success you attained by using the new approach.

Life now looks like this – Paint a picture of how life and business improved after the solution.

Social Proof – Provide examples of how others have also achieved success with the same method or product, reinforcing its value.

Chapter Twenty-Three

Bundling Idiot Or Bundling Success?

Bundling Idiot Or Bundling Success?

Mike Martin sat in his small, cluttered office, surrounded by papers, telephones, and a constant hum of frustration. He was the sales guy for Lead Simplify—a company that had developed what Mike believed to be the greatest product ever invented. Lead Simplify was a game-changer; it automated the collection, distribution, and sale of leads for businesses, but no one seemed to get it. The market didn't really exist for such a product, and potential customers were confused by its purpose.

Mike's frustration grew as he watched competitors rely on traditional call networks or pay-per-conversion platforms, missing out on the potential profit his software could provide. He had tried every angle to sell Lead Simplify as a lead sales platform, but every pitch fell flat. No one was interested.

Mike had poured his heart into developing this product with his business partner, Martyn. It all started when Martyn had walked into Mike's office one day, finding him juggling two telephones, a payment terminal, and two notepads. One notepad contained a list of engineers and contractors who would take jobs from Mike. The other was a ledger for taking booking fees from customers or payments from contractors. Mike was frantically managing the business manually—answering calls, dispatching jobs, and processing payments.

Martyn saw the chaos and had an idea: "We can automate this," he had said, and thus, Lead Simplify was born. The software was designed to do exactly what Mike was doing, but on autopilot. It had the potential to save businesses time and money.

But despite its potential, Lead Simplify was a tough sell. Business owners just couldn't see the value. They already had an "easy" way out with their existing methods, even if it wasn't making them much money. The sales pitches felt like talking to a brick wall. No one seemed to grasp the value of the product.

Weeks turned into months, and the frustration only deepened. Mike knew he needed to do something different. He needed to find a way to show potential customers not just what Lead Simplify was, but what it could do for them. The problem was, the market didn't know it needed Lead Simplify—yet.

Mike began to question himself. "Why can't they see it?" he thought. "Why don't they understand how much money they could make? How much time they could save?" The answer wasn't clear. He realised that simply explaining the product wasn't enough. He had to show them how it could change their business.

Mike went on a rampage, searching through endless books, articles, and webinars. He watched and studied other entrepreneurs who had faced similar challenges. He knew there had to be a strategy out there that could work. He needed to change his approach.

One night, while watching a webinar, something clicked. The speaker was an entrepreneur who had faced a similar issue—selling a product in a non-existent market. The key to his success? Bundling. By offering a package of products and services together, he created a solution that felt complete and irresistible to his customers.

The more Mike thought about bundling, the more it made sense. He realised that business owners weren't just buying software; they were buying a solution to their problem. But for them to see Lead Simplify as the solution, it needed to come packaged with everything they could possibly need to achieve their goals. It wasn't just about selling software anymore; it was about selling a complete roadmap to success.

Mike needed to think beyond Lead Simplify. What else did his customers need? What would make the package so valuable, so irresistible, that they couldn't help but buy it? He needed to create a bundle that covered every aspect of their journey—from where they were now to where they wanted to be.

He imagined a potential customer sitting at their desk, overwhelmed by managing leads, scheduling jobs, and handling payments. What if Lead Simplify came with a bundle of tools that automated not just lead management, but also marketing, customer follow-up, and reporting? What if it included training sessions on how to optimise their business processes, plus 24/7 support to help them every step of the way?

Mike's mind raced with possibilities. He realised that if he could package all these elements together, he could create a comprehensive solution that felt like an absolute no-brainer.

Mike got to work, designing the ultimate bundle. He called it the "Lead Simplify Success Package." It wasn't just Lead Simplify software; it was a complete ecosystem. The package included:

Lead Simplify Software: For automating lead management and sales.

Marketing Automation Tool Magic Page Plug-in: To help businesses drive more leads.

Customer Follow-Up System: Ensuring no lead was ever left unattended.

Training Modules: Step-by-step guides on optimising business processes.

24/7 Support and Consultation: Direct access to experts to help customers at any time.

The bundle was designed to take a business owner from start to finish, covering every possible need they might have. And here was the kicker: buying all these elements separately would cost a fortune. But as part of the "Lead Simplify Success Package," customers could get everything for a fraction of the cost if they paid annually.

Mike knew he needed to make this offer feel urgent, so he added a limited-time discount for the first 100 customers. This created a sense of urgency and exclusivity, making the deal even more attractive.

He reached out to his network, scheduled webinars, and updated the website with the new package. The transformation was immediate. Suddenly, business owners were not just interested—they were excited. They could see the value clearly. They could see the entire roadmap from where they were to where they wanted to be.

Within weeks, the sales numbers began to climb. Orders poured in as customers jumped on the opportunity to get everything they needed in one go. Mike couldn't believe it. Lead Simplify had finally found its footing in the market.

Bundling transformed Mike's approach to selling Lead Simplify. By understanding his customers' complete journey and offering them a comprehensive solution, he turned a struggling product into a must-have package. The success of Lead Simplify wasn't just about the software; it was about understanding what his customers needed, bundling those solutions together, and offering them an irresistible deal.

And from that moment on, Lead Simplify never looked back.

Lesson: Sometimes, it's not about selling a product; it's about selling a solution. And when you package that solution just right, customers can't help but say yes.

Chapter Twenty-Four

Make Them Emotional

Make Them Emotional

Simon stared blankly at the bathroom mirror, studying his own reflection. He sighed heavily, his shoulders slumping as he tugged at the collar of his ill-fitting suit. The suit, much like his life, was worn out and barely holding together. At 53, Simon was far from the picture of health. His once-thick hair had thinned to a few wispy strands that he futilely tried to comb over his balding head. His belly spilled over his belt, a constant reminder of the stress eating that had become his nightly routine. His skin, pale and blotchy, told stories of a man who spent more time in his car than under the sun.

Simon was a life insurance salesman, and not a very good one at that. Every day, he knocked on doors, carrying a briefcase full of policy papers and a heart full of desperation. His job was simple: get inside, explain the policy, and ask if they wanted to buy. But the truth was, Simon didn't believe in his own pitch. He found it hard to muster enthusiasm for a product that promised so little in the present and only delivered after someone had kicked the bucket.

His colleagues were no help. The top salespeople in the company—smooth, charismatic, and full of confidence—guarded their secrets like treasure. They had their scripts, their smiles, and their strategies, but they never shared. Simon, on the other hand, clung to the company-provided script like a life raft. It was dry, mechanical, and utterly devoid of emotion. And it was getting him nowhere.

Month after month, Simon's numbers were dismal. In his first month, he made four sales—half of his target. The next month, five. His boss had given him a stern warning: "Twenty-four sales per quarter, or you're out." Simon was on nine, with just one month to go. He needed fifteen more sales, or he'd be sacked. At his age, with his health, finding another job was unlikely. Without the job, the mortgage would go unpaid, the bills would pile up, and his family—his wife, his teenage daughter—would suffer.

His wife, Mary, tried to reassure him. "You're new, Simon. Give it time. You'll get the hang of it." But time was not on his side. The pressure mounted, and with each passing day, Simon felt the crushing weight of impending failure.

One morning, as he sat in his car, nervously tapping the steering wheel, he remembered an old friend—Jack. Jack was a sales legend, a master of persuasion who'd made millions and travelled the world sharing his sales wisdom. They hadn't seen each other in years, but they had arranged to meet for lunch the following week. Simon hoped against hope that Jack might have the answer to his problems.

When the day finally came, Simon arrived at the restaurant early. He fidgeted with his tie, wiped his clammy hands on his trousers, and tried to steady his nerves. Jack arrived in a flash of confidence and charisma—a tall, fit man with a broad smile and an infectious laugh. They exchanged pleasantries, catching up on old times, but Simon's mind was elsewhere. As they sat down to eat, he knew he had to ask for Jack's help.

Taking a deep breath, Simon blurted out, "Jack, I'm in a bit of a predicament. I could really use your advice."

Jack's eyes narrowed, concern flickering across his face. "What's going on, mate?"

Simon explained his situation—the missed targets, the looming deadline, the risk of losing his job. He poured his heart out, hoping Jack might have a magic bullet, some secret script or tactic that could turn things around.

Jack listened intently, then leaned back in his chair, a sly smile spreading across his face. "Simon, you're going about this all wrong," he said. "You're selling life insurance as if it's a product. It's not. It's a lifeline, a promise. You're not selling policies, mate. You're selling peace of mind."

Simon blinked, confused. "I don't understand. What do you mean?"

Jack leaned in, lowering his voice. "Let me ask you something, Simon. If you died tomorrow, what would happen to your children?"

Simon was taken aback. "Why would you ask me that?" he stammered.

"Just answer the question," Jack pressed. "If you died tomorrow, what would happen?"

"Well... they'd stay with Mary," Simon said slowly.

"And what would happen to Mary?" Jack continued, his eyes locked onto Simon's.

Simon shifted uncomfortably in his seat. "She... she'd struggle. Financially. Emotionally. She'd have to take care of the kids, maybe get a part-time job. It would be hard."

Jack nodded. "And your life insurance—how much is it worth?"

"Three hundred thousand," Simon muttered. "The mortgage would be paid off, but that's about it."

Jack leaned back, a satisfied smile on his face. "Are you okay with that? Leaving your family to struggle like that?"

Simon's heart sank. He hadn't thought about it like this. "No... no, I'm not okay with that."

"Then why haven't you increased your coverage? Why haven't you made sure they're taken care of if something happens to you?" Jack's voice was firm, almost accusing.

Simon was silent, the weight of Jack's words settling on him. Suddenly, it clicked. Jack had just sold him. Not on a product, but on an idea, a feeling. He'd made him feel the fear, the guilt, the urgency.

Jack grinned. "That's how you sell life insurance, Simon. You make it personal. You find out what they care about most—their family, their future—and you tap into that. You don't sell them a policy; you sell them peace of mind. Security. The knowledge that their loved ones will be okay."

Simon nodded slowly, the lesson sinking in. "I think I get it now. It's about making an emotional connection, isn't it?"

"Exactly," Jack said, leaning back. "Forget the script. Forget the numbers. Talk to them. Find out what keeps them up at night. Make them feel the fear of loss, the relief of security. You do that, and you'll sell every time."

The next day, Simon didn't go straight to his appointments. Instead, he spent the morning rethinking his entire approach. He scribbled notes, watched videos on emotional selling, and practised his new pitch in front of the mirror. When he finally hit the road, he felt something he hadn't felt in a long time—hope.

At his first appointment, he didn't open with the usual script. Instead, he asked, "What's the most important thing in your life?" The couple across the table looked surprised, but soon they were talking about their children, their dreams, their fears. Simon listened intently, nodding, empathising, and when the time was right, he asked, "And if something happened to you tomorrow, would they be okay?"

By the end of the meeting, he had his first sale of the day. And by the end of the week, he had more than doubled his usual numbers. Each time, he dug deep, connecting with his clients on an emotional level, making them see not just the policy, but the promise behind it.

Within six months, Simon was the top salesman in the company, earning more than he ever had before. His family was secure, his confidence soared, and he had Jack to thank for it. All it took was one lunch, one conversation, to change everything.

Lesson: People make decisions emotionally first and justify them later with logic.

Chapter Twenty-Five

Empathy, Not Sympathy

Empathy, Not Sympathy

J ack Weston had been a cosmetic surgery consultant for over a year now. He was young, fit, and had a natural charm that could make most clients feel at ease. His toned physique was something he was proud of, and he often used it as a silent testament to his disciplined lifestyle. But today, as he sat across from his new client, he could sense something different.

Rebecca was a woman in her mid-thirties, slightly hunched over, dressed in a baggy jumper that swallowed her frame. Her eyes darted nervously around the room, avoiding Jack's gaze. She was here for a consultation about body contouring, but the way she spoke, Jack could tell this wasn't just about a bit of excess weight.

"Rebecca," Jack began, using his usual upbeat tone, "I can assure you, this procedure is very straightforward. Our clients often see immediate results, and it's a fantastic way to feel more confident in your own skin."

Rebecca looked down, her fingers nervously twisting the corner of her sleeve. "I just... I don't know," she murmured. "I'm terrified. It's not just the surgery... it's... it's how I feel..."

Jack, misunderstanding her hesitation, continued with his pitch. "I completely understand. Surgery can be daunting, but our team is top-notch. And think about how much better you'll feel afterwards. You could finally show off that beautiful body of yours!"

Rebecca flinched slightly. "Show off?" she whispered, her voice almost breaking. "I don't want to show off, I just... I just don't want to be scared anymore..."

Jack was used to clients feeling apprehensive, but this felt different. He had always believed in the power of a strong, confident approach. Show them how great they could look, focus on the results, and the rest would follow. But Rebecca wasn't biting. In fact, she seemed to be retreating even more into herself.

He could see the unease in her eyes. She was shifting in her seat, her breathing getting shallower. Jack realised he was losing her. His usual tactics weren't working.

"Look," he said, trying another angle, "I know this might be hard to imagine, but think of how you'll feel when you can walk into any room and just... own it."

Rebecca's eyes welled up with tears. "I don't want to own any room," she said, her voice trembling. "I just want to not hate myself when I look in the mirror. I want to not cry when I try on clothes. I want to go to the beach with my kids without feeling like a monster."

Jack was taken aback. His mind raced. He had dealt with body dysmorphia cases before, but he realised now he had never truly understood the depth of the pain. He had always approached it with a clinical mindset—identify the problem, suggest the solution, close the sale. But here was a woman who was living a nightmare every day, trapped in a body she despised, and he was treating it like just another sales opportunity.

He leaned back, feeling a pang of guilt. He had been focusing on the wrong thing. He had been seeing Rebecca as a potential client, not a person in pain.

Rebecca stood up abruptly. "I think I've made a mistake coming here," she said, turning towards the door. "I'm sorry for wasting your time."

Jack's heart sank. He knew he had blown it. As Rebecca reached for the door, something in him shifted. He saw a reflection of himself in the glass pane—his toned arms, his chiselled jawline, his perfect image.

And suddenly, he was flooded with a memory he hadn't thought about in years.

"Rebecca, wait," he called out. She paused, her hand on the door handle, but didn't turn around.

"Please, just give me a moment," he said softly. "I want to tell you something."

She hesitated, then turned slightly, her eyes still avoiding his.

Jack took a deep breath. "I know I may not seem like the right person to understand what you're going through. I mean, look at me now. But two years ago, I was a very different man. I was 18 stone, and I couldn't even look at myself in the mirror without feeling disgusted. I hated my body, hated myself. I wouldn't go to the beach, wouldn't go swimming with my kids—I felt like I didn't deserve to enjoy life."

Rebecca looked up, surprise flickering in her eyes.

"I decided to have the surgery because I was at my wit's end," Jack continued. "But it wasn't just the surgery that changed me. It was what it represented. For the first time in my life, I saw a glimpse of what could be, a version of myself I could actually like.

And that motivated me to keep going, to keep making better choices, to take care of myself—not because I wanted to show off, but because I wanted to live without that constant fear, that self-hate."

Rebecca's grip on the door handle loosened. She turned fully to face him now. There was a softness in her eyes, a tentative hope.

Jack took a step closer, his voice gentle but firm. "I'm not here to sell you a fantasy, Rebecca. I'm here because I know what it's like to feel trapped in your own skin. And I want you to know that it's okay to feel that way. It's okay to be scared. But you don't have to face it alone. We can take this journey together, at your pace. And I promise, we'll do everything we can to help you feel better—not just on the outside, but on the inside too."

Rebecca's eyes filled with tears again, but this time, they weren't tears of fear or frustration. They were tears of relief. She nodded slowly. "Thank you," she whispered. "Thank you for understanding."

Jack smiled softly. "It's my job," he said. "But more than that, it's my privilege to help you see yourself the way you deserve to be seen."

Rebecca took a deep breath, her posture relaxing for the first time since she walked in. She stepped away from the door and back towards the chair, her eyes finally meeting Jack's with a glimmer of trust.

And as she sat down, ready to listen, Jack knew he had finally found the key to making a real difference. Not by selling an image, but by showing empathy—by truly understanding and connecting with the person sitting across from him.

He had learned that sometimes, the best way to help someone change their reflection in the mirror was to first change the reflection in their heart.

Lesson: Empathy in sales isn't just about understanding the customer's problem; it's about connecting with them on a human level. When you show genuine empathy, you build trust, and that trust can turn a hesitant prospect into a lifelong client. Remember, it's not just about the sale; it's about making a real difference in someone's life.

Chapter Twenty-Six

The Eight Commandments

The Eight Commandments

Mike had been in sales for nearly a decade, working for a company he could no longer stand. At first, he had been drawn in by the allure of big commissions and the promise of rapid advancement. But over the years, he had watched as his company repeatedly deceived its customers, hid its mistakes, and prioritised profit over people.

If a product was faulty, they'd blame the customer or the supplier. If a delivery was late, they'd point fingers at the courier service. There was no accountabil-ity, no transparency. Mike felt like he was constantly lying, making excuses, or keeping secrets.

The company didn't just lack integrity—they were allergic to it. There was never a sense of owning up to mistakes, and whenever a client raised an issue, it was swiftly brushed under the rug or met with a half-hearted apology. Mike's colleagues were trained to dodge responsibility, to pivot to the next sale with-out a thought for the damage left in their wake.

After years of this, Mike reached a breaking point. He couldn't stand the dishonesty any longer. He knew he was better than this, that sales didn't have to be about manipulation and deceit. One Friday af-ternoon, after yet another heated argument with his boss about "playing the game," Mike decided he'd had enough. He handed in his resignation.

Walking out of the office for the last time, a sense of relief washed over him. He felt like a weight had been lifted off his shoulders. But as the relief settled, another feeling began to grow: determination. Mike didn't want to just walk away from sales; he wanted to prove that there was another way, a better way.

The Birth of the Eight Commandments

Mike decided to start his own business in the same industry. But this time, he would do things differently. He grabbed a notebook and began jotting down what he called his "Eight Commandments"—a set of principles he would commit to, no matter what. He was determined to build a business rooted in trust, transparency, and integrity.

He wrote down:

1. **Consistency**: Always deliver on promises and meet deadlines.

2. **Transparency**: Be upfront and honest about all processes, policies, and potential issues.

3. **Integrity**: Act with honesty and ethical standards, even when it's not the easiest or most profitable route.

4. **Responsiveness**: Address customer concerns and questions promptly.

5. **Personalisation**: Understand the customer's needs and preferences and cater to them as individuals.

6. **Reliability**: Ensure products and services consistently perform as expected.

7. **Accountability**: Take responsibility when things go wrong and make it right.

8. **Security**: Protect customer data and privacy, reassuring them that their information is safe.

Mike took these Eight Commandments and framed them, placing them prominently in his home office. They were his guiding principles, the foundation upon which he would build his new venture.

As Mike launched his business, he encountered challenges. The market was competitive, and he was up against some of the same companies he'd previously worked for, including his old employer. He knew they would use every trick in the book to win over clients. But Mike had something they didn't: trust.

Every time a potential client expressed hesitation or doubt, Mike would direct them to his Eight Commandments. "This is how I do business," he'd say.

"These are the values I stand by." And then he'd tell them stories—real stories—of times when he could have taken the easy way out but chose instead to follow his commandments.

There was the time when a shipment got delayed due to a supplier error. Rather than blame the supplier, Mike took full responsibility, informed the client immediately, and provided a discount for the inconvenience. Or the time a product failed shortly after delivery. Instead of denying fault, he apologised, replaced the product without question, and added a free service upgrade. Each story reinforced the idea that his company was different.

And the clients responded. They appreciated his honesty, his willingness to admit mistakes, and his commitment to making things right. Word began to spread about this new company that was upfront, reliable, and trustworthy.

Months went by, and Mike's business started to grow. He realised that the Eight Commandments weren't just a set of rules; they were a powerful marketing tool. He decided to take a bold step: he put the

Eight Commandments on the homepage of his website. No flashy sales talk, no exaggerated claims—just his values and what they meant for his customers.

He ran a new ad campaign, but instead of directing people to a landing page filled with offers and deals, he sent them straight to the page with his Eight Commandments. And the response was overwhelming. Clients began reaching out, not because they were drawn in by flashy ads, but because they resonated with the honesty and integrity they saw.

Some would call and say, "I've been burned before by companies who promised the world but delivered nothing. I'm tired of the lies. I want to work with someone I can trust."

Others would share their own horror stories of dealing with businesses that operated like Mike's old company, companies that only cared about the next sale.

Every time Mike heard these stories, he was reminded of why he'd left his old job in the first place. He wasn't just selling products; he was selling trust.

Within a year, Mike's company had more than doubled in size. He had a loyal base of clients who not only came back time and again but also referred their friends, family, and business contacts. His competitors, including his old employer, couldn't understand it. They were baffled by how a new company could be doing so well without resorting to their underhanded tactics.

But Mike knew the secret: trust.

By sticking to his Eight Commandments, he built a business where customers felt valued, heard, and respected. He didn't need to hide behind excuses or blame others for mistakes. And because of that, his clients stayed.

As Mike looked around his thriving business, he felt a deep sense of satisfaction. He had proven that there was a better way to do sales—a way that prioritised people over profits, integrity over deceit, and long-term relationships over quick wins.

He glanced at the framed Eight Commandments on his wall and smiled. They weren't just words; they were the foundation of everything he'd built, a testament to what could be achieved when trust was the guiding principle.

And that was something no dodgy company could ever compete with.

Lesson: Follow the eight commandments:

1. **Consistency**: Always deliver on promises and meet deadlines.

2. **Transparency**: Be upfront and honest about all processes, policies, and potential issues.

3. **Integrity**: Act with honesty and ethical standards, even when it's not the easiest or most profitable route.

4. **Responsiveness**: Address customer concerns and questions promptly.

5. **Personalisation**: Understand the customer's needs and preferences and cater to them as individuals.

6. **Reliability**: Ensure products and services consistently perform as expected.

7. **Accountability**: Take responsibility when things go wrong and make it right.

8. **Security**: Protect customer data and privacy, reassuring them that their information is safe.

Thank you for reading my book. I hope this helps you and your sales team become better salespeople.

Mike Martin: *"Proud to be a salesman"*

https://mikemartin.uk

Printed in Great Britain
by Amazon